"Kathy Miller Perkins is a pioneer in studying how organizational culture and leadership affects a company's sustainability efforts. Her rare combination of research skills and years of practical experience have made this book a useful guide for any business leader looking to integrate sustainability issues in corporate strategy."

George Serafeim, *Professor of Business Administration at Harvard Business School*

"Kathy Miller Perkins' work on culture, sustainability and purpose remains seminal. From her groundbreaking analysis on organizational culture performed with Eccles and Serafeim, up through this critically important new book, she is always one to watch. The culture and purpose of organizations couldn't be more important in this age of ever increasing environmental and social challenge. Here's hoping this insightful new book inspires more organizations to join those already on board for this critically important ride."

Cary Krosinsky, *Lecturer at Yale and Brown University*

"As a professional in workplace design, I believe in aligning business purpose, culture and workplace environment. This book presents strong arguments for why leaders should care about signaling what they stand for. Through tips, tools and colorful stories, Kathy Miller Perkins shows readers how to create a culture and environment that inspires people while supporting business purpose and long-term success."

Jack E. Weber, *IIDA, MCR, LEED AP, Senior Vice President/Design Principal, Gresham Smith*

"Kathleen Miller Perkins provides a very valuable tool for any 21st century manager who wants to create long-term value for the firm and for society. Based on 200 interviews of executives in 60 companies, Kathleen has written an imminently readable text, full of examples and self-guided workbook exercises. Any progressive manager should read this book."

Dr. Tima Bansal, *Ivey Business School, Canada Research Chair in Business, Sustainability*

"This book is THE handbook for any leader committed to creating a sustainable business culture designed for the next decade. The material is accessible and engaging, with practical tips and tools woven with memorable case studies from Kathy's many years of research. I recommend this for any leader aspiring to create a purpose driven organization."

Anne Chambers, *Co-Founder, Certifiably*

"At Dow our purpose inspires and guides everything that we do. And the right culture enables us to live our purpose. This book provides a roadmap for leaders who wish to build a culture where every employee contributes to the company's bottom line while also making a difference in the world. I have worked with Kathy Miller Perkins and can vouch for the value she brings to leaders through her solid research and practical tips and tools."

"How can I lead my organization towards long-term success? How can I find a work with purpose? Can I change my company's culture? If these questions keep you up at night, then *Leadership and Purpose* is a must read. As an incredibly thoughtful and experienced practitioner working with purpose-driven organizations, Kathy provides tools to support change and enable the development of sustainable organizational cultures."

"The further companies go on the journey of integrating sustainability into their business, the more it becomes clear to me that purpose, culture and leadership are *the* essential ingredients to move forward. Kathy's work with Brown-Forman in the early days of deepening and advancing our sustainability commitment helped put us on a path to better understand and leverage culture, purpose and employee engagement. Like a fine cocktail, this book provides just the right mix of thought leadership, research, guidance and tools to accelerate sustainability progress."

Leadership and Purpose

Companies that have integrated a contribution to society into their business models are more likely than others to succeed for the long term. This book provides you with information, tips, and tools to assess and strengthen your company for ongoing success.

Through the use of case studies, the book describes the leaders' journeys – the mistakes they made, the successes they achieved, and the lessons they learned. Some are certified as Benefits Corporations (B Corps) because they have incorporated a clear societal purpose into their missions and they are able to demonstrate positive social impact. Others, while not certified B Corps, are at various stages in their commitments to society.

The book is for leaders at many levels, including CEOs, senior leaders, and managers, as well as those without formal positions of authority but who can influence others and contribute to a sustainable culture.

Kathleen Miller Perkins is a social psychologist, consultant, teacher, writer, and researcher. For over 35 years she has worked with both national and international clients in areas such as leading change, developing sustainable organizational culture, collaborating across boundaries, and developing leaders. She has served on the faculty of the Center for Leadership in Global Sustainability, Virginia Tech, USA, and the Business School of Lausanne, Switzerland.

Leadership and Purpose

How to Create a Sustainable Culture

Kathleen Miller Perkins

Routledge
Taylor & Francis Group

LONDON AND NEW YORK

First published 2020
by Routledge
2 Park Square, Milton Park, Abingdon, Oxon OX14 4RN

and by Routledge
52 Vanderbilt Avenue, New York, NY 10017

Routledge is an imprint of the Taylor & Francis Group, an informa business

British Library Cataloguing-in-Publication Data
A catalogue record for this book is available from the British Library

Library of Congress Cataloging-in-Publication Data
Names: Perkins, Kathleen Miller, author.
Title: Leadership and purpose : how to create a sustainable culture /
    Kathleen Miller Perkins.
Description: Abingdon, Oxon ; New York, NY : Routledge, 2019.
Identifiers: LCCN 2019003327| ISBN 9780367217693 (hardback)
    | ISBN 9780367243982 (pbk.) | ISBN 9780429265952
    (ebook)
Subjects: LCSH: Social responsibility of business. | Sustainable
    development. | Corporate culture.
Classification: LCC HD60 .P425 2019 | DDC 658.4/092—dc23
LC record available at https://lccn.loc.gov/2019003327

ISBN: 978-0-367-21769-3 (hbk)
ISBN: 978-0-429-26595-2 (ebk)

Typeset in Bembo
by Swales & Willis Ltd, Exeter, Devon, UK

Printed and bound in Great Britain by
TJ International Ltd, Padstow, Cornwall

I would like to dedicate this book to my mother who taught me that living with purpose is the only way to live.

Contents

Developing the capacity for transformational change 150
Summary and conclusions 153
Your turn: assessing your company 153

Foreword

Each organization, its leaders, members, and external stakeholders must make a fundamental decision: Do they exist for the benefit of society or does society exist for the benefit of them? Can and should their organization operate outside of and with complete disregard for the places where it does its business, as an economic engine beholden only to the economic interests of its various stakeholders?

Those organizations that operate with the assumption that they have a responsibility to society pursue a purpose beyond profits. They are building bridges by which societies can be sustained. Purpose is not only good for business but is a necessary ingredient for the longevity of societies – arguments that Kathy Miller Perkins also makes throughout this book. For the past ten years she has studied how organizations build cultures to support their purpose. And, based on her research and consulting experiences, she has written this book which offers sound evidence and practical advice for leaders.

Kathy and I met while exploring with a group of artists, business leaders, and academics what leadership will look like for the next decade. Kathy and I found that we shared a common commitment to digging into thorny questions critical to my work with the Center for Creative Leadership and her research and consulting practice around sustainability and corporate culture. After our initial meeting, we worked together through the Virginia Tech's Center for Leadership in Global Sustainability (CLiGS) where we engaged students and fellow faculty members in probing related issues. Through these common experiences, I came to know Kathy well and to recognize the significance of her work in helping leaders understand and create cultures to support their organizations' purpose and values.

Evidence-based advice is rare, high quality longitudinal study even rarer. In this context, the deep evidence-based advice and practical tools regarding purpose, organizations, and their cultures that Kathy provides could hardly be more important, not only to organizations but to the societies in which they operate. Purpose cannot be responsibly ignored, and neither can Kathy's work.

Jerry Abrams,
Envisioneer at the Center for Creative Leadership and Senior Fellow
with the Center for Leadership in Global Sustainability

Preface

I have been interested in culture for my entire professional career. Since my graduate school days, I have been curious about the factors that influence how we think and act and how groups of people develop shared beliefs that feed a culture. Over time my focus turned to organizational cultures. Through my ongoing research and my consulting practice I have explored how cultures develop and what maintains them. And perhaps more importantly, what, if anything, can lead an organization to change.

I developed an interest in sustainable cultures approximately ten years ago. I was helping a hydroelectric company prepare for major change when I heard the phrases triple bottom line and sustainability – concepts that meant little to me at the time. Nevertheless, before long I could see these commitments to the environment, social issues, and finance figured prominently in their corporate identity and decision-making. I was intrigued and wanted to learn more.

Over the last decade I have worked with many companies committed to sustainability. Their reasons vary. Some aim to save money. Others seek a way to burnish their reputations. But the ones that truly inspired me wanted to make a positive contribution to society. As I worked with them I began to notice a consistent pattern in their cultures. I was interested in the role that these somewhat unique cultures played in what seemed to be superior performance. I wrote this book to share with you what I have learned in hopes that you can apply the lessons to your own companies.

Acknowledgments

I would like to thank my husband Steve for helping me sort out my own muddled thoughts, for challenging me when I didn't always welcome it, for encouraging me when I said I would never finish this book, and for spending endless hours reading, editing, and suggesting. And thanks to my administrative assistant Cecilia Stephens for her assistance and patience.

Thanks to Robert Eccles and George Serafeim for their work on the early research which led to the refinement of the culture assessment instrument SCALA™ and the development of the first model for how to become a sustainable company.

Thank you to Meredith Wells Lepley for her tireless statistical analyses and her valuable contributions to the interpretations of the data. Thanks also to the DBA students at the Business School of Lausanne (BSL) who invited companies to participate in our work and administered the SCALA to those companies.

And finally, thanks to all the people in our client companies with whom I have worked over the years. Together we have tackled complex challenges and I have learned much from them in the process. And, as a bonus, I have developed lasting relationships with many.

Introduction

When I started my company 30 plus years ago, I had a vision. I wanted to help other organizations succeed by enabling creative people to make valuable contributions through meaningful work. As a social psychologist I was most interested in organizational cultures and how they could enable companies to thrive. These many years later, I am still pursuing the same purpose. The difference now is that seeking a purpose beyond profit is significantly more common in the corporate world.

More and more leaders are realizing that if they want their businesses to survive for the long term they must balance the pursuit of profits with a commitment to contribute to society. And as they follow this path, they are finding that the rewards are more than merely monetary. The personal satisfaction and pride in the company that comes from carrying out a greater purpose is truly priceless. My work with clients over the decades has led me to conclude that passion follows purpose. When people believe that their work is contributing to their company's success and to the greater good in society, they are more engaged.

I have learned that it takes a certain kind of culture to support the balance of purpose and profits. Throughout this book I will refer to these cultures as sustainable. And they don't emerge by accident. Ensuring that the conditions are right for sustainable cultures to develop requires insight, resolve, and hard work. Throughout this book I share the lessons that I have learned from our work with client organizations as well as from leading my own company to become more sustainable. I describe what a sustainable culture looks like and how to think about and strengthen your own company culture as you too pursue purpose and profits.

Why you should read this book

None of us has the crystal ball that enables us to see into the future. Yet we want to lead our companies towards long-term success. We know that the context for business success is becoming increasingly complex. Conditions can shift very quickly whether we are ready or not. We function in a world where borders tend to be fluid and information is readily available to anyone who wishes to access it. The world's many economies are intertwined such that the successes or failures of one often impact the others. We are threatened by climate change, human rights violations, and scarce natural resources. Thus, all of us must prepare our companies for a future where circumstances are constantly evolving. And organizational culture has a key role to play. This book is based on research that uncovers the characteristics of cultures that can support our companies' long-term viability in these challenging times.

You should read this book to reflect on your company and the role that you can play to ensure that it not only remains viable but also contributes to the well-being of the world over the long term. The right organizational culture can provide your company with a strategic advantage currently and into the future. This book will guide you through an assessment of your current culture and will provide you with tips and tools to strengthen it.

The purpose of this book

The purpose of this book is to provide you with resources for assessing and strengthening your organization's culture to support your company's ongoing success. Throughout the book I argue the following: Companies that have integrated a contribution to society into their business models are more likely than others to last for the long term. I refer to them as sustainable companies. I present evidence, both research and experiential, to support this claim. Based on a ten-year research program and my own practical on-the-ground experiences, I present the characteristics of sustainable cultures – those that best support sustainable companies.

Throughout this book you will read about companies with varying approaches to fulfilling social responsibilities. Some are certified as Benefits Corporations (B Corps) because they have incorporated a clear societal purpose into their missions and they are able to demonstrate positive social impact. Others, while not certified B Corps, are at various stages in their commitments to society. Through case studies, I will share leaders' journeys – the mistakes they made, the successes they achieved, and the lessons they learned.

Who should read this book

I have written this book for leaders at many levels, including CEOs, senior leaders, and managers. However, I also speak to people without formal positions of authority who, nevertheless, can influence others and contribute to a sustainable culture. We can all have an impact on our organizations' cultures and our companies' futures.

While I have had many roles over the course of my career, I am a practitioner first. For many years I have worked on the ground with organizational culture and the people-side of change. Throughout this book I will provide you with information and tools that I have used successfully in my own work and that you can apply in your companies as you lead them to become more sustainable.

Overview of research methods

All the material in this book is based on research. I have reviewed available research reports and articles extensively and have incorporated the relevant findings. In addition, I have included results from my own team's research. We have administered the survey assessment instrument that my company developed and validated, the SCALA™ (Sustainable Culture and Leadership Assessment), in many of our studies. I present greater detail about the instrument and the research in the Appendix.

I began conducting this research when leaders in a client organization asked my company to help them understand how their culture was affecting their ability to create and successfully execute a long-term sustainability strategy. After we completed this project, I joined a research team with Robert Eccles, Professor of Management Practice, Harvard Business School, and George Serafeim, Professor of Business Administration, Harvard Business School. At the time, Bob and George were studying how companies could better integrate sustainability into the core of their strategy and operations while I was studying culture and sustainability. We conducted over 200 interviews in more than 60 companies. As patterns emerged related to leadership and culture, we developed and tested a survey instrument. The results of our work with that instrument showed the specific characteristics that differentiated companies with strong sustainability outcomes from those with weaker results.[1] Subsequently my company has administered the assessment instrument, the SCALA™, to over 4,000 people in 200+ organizations around the world.

Over the past few years, I have worked with Meredith Lepley, faculty member of the University of Southern California, in studying patterns across our entire data base. And recently we have joined Katrin Muff, former Dean of the Business School of Lausanne, and Agnieszka Kapalka, research associate at the Business School of Lausanne, in studying companies that are not only sustainable but are also clearly purpose-driven.[2]

Definitions

Words such as *leader, culture, sustainable, sustainability*, and *purpose-driven* can be confusing because their meanings vary. Therefore, I would like to define how I will use the terms in this book.

Leaders

Those who can influence others with or without a formal position of authority.

Purpose-driven company

A company with clear intentions to run the business by balancing purpose and profits. The purpose, which can include either social or environmental commitments or both, is integrated into their business models and strategies.

Sustainable company (or socially responsible company)

Companies that sustain competitive advantage for the long term by integrating a contribution to society into their business models. These companies show strong performance in the following areas: Financial, environmental, social, and governance. In this book the expression *sustainable company* is interchangeable with *socially responsible company* and *sustainability*.

Sustainability

A company's ability to sustain competitive advantage over the long term through strong financial performance and the integration of environmental, social, and governance factors into the core of the company's strategy and operations. This definition reflects how we have defined the terms in our research. In this book the term *sustainability* is interchangeable with the definitions of *sustainable company* and *socially responsible company*.

Organizational culture

Collective beliefs, attitudes, and behaviors concerning issues such as why the company exists, what it stands for, how people within it should act, how employees and external stakeholders are treated.

Sustainable culture

An organizational culture that supports purpose-driven, sustainable companies.

Organization of the content

The book is divided into the following three parts.

Part I: fundamentals

The purpose of Part I is to review the fundamentals of sustainable companies and sustainable cultures. Chapter 1 includes an overview of why becoming sustainable is important. I present a profile of a sustainable company in this chapter along with charts that show the specific qualities that differentiate them from others. The subsequent chapters cover the three fundamental building blocks of culture: Leadership, identity, and trust.

Chapter 2 examines what leadership looks like in sustainable companies. Chapter 3 focuses on a company's identity, meaning how people within view it and how they wish others to see it. This chapter looks at how the unique identities of sustainable companies develop. Finally, Chapter 4 considers the role of trust in an organization's culture. The chapter examines how both interpersonal and organizational trust influence every other aspect of the organizational culture.

Part II: the nature of sustainable cultures

The purpose of Part II is to provide more detail on the aspects of culture that rest on the fundamental building blocks described in Part I. Chapter 5 explores how internal organizational culture supports the purpose of sustainable companies. Chapter 6 looks at the nature of the relationships that people inside an organization have with those on the outside. This chapter includes a discussion of how sustainable companies collaborate with others and describes the factors that determine the success of these endeavors. Chapter 7 reviews what it means for a company to be change-adept. The chapter presents the arguments for why becoming change-adept is critical for all organizations, and especially for sustainable companies. This chapter discusses why sustainable companies tend to have better track records for change.

Part III: deep change

The purpose of Part III is to explore *how* companies change to become sustainable. Chapter 8 looks at mental models or the lens through which we view our experiences and how they enable or hinder change and transformation. This chapter highlights how the mental models of sustainable companies differ from others. Chapter 9 presents a model for how to become a sustainable company. The chapter examines the Transformational Cycle model and describes each stage that comprises it. Subsequently the chapter explores transformational change in greater detail as well as what it requires of leaders.

Notes

1 R.G. Eccles, K. Miller Perkins and G. Serafeim, "How to Become a Sustainable Company," *MIT Sloan Management Review* 53, no. 4 (summer 2012): 43–50.
2 For a more complete overview of the research methodologies, see the Appendix.

Part I

Fundamentals

The purpose of Part I is to introduce the fundamentals of sustainable companies and sustainable cultures. In the first chapter, I present the arguments for why all companies should become sustainable, performing across three dimensions: Environmental, social, and financial. The chapter introduces the topics that I cover in greater detail throughout the book. It includes a profile of a sustainable company along with a description of the qualities that differentiate them from others. The subsequent chapters in Part I explore the three fundamental building blocks of culture in sustainable companies: Leadership, identity, and trust. Chapter 2 considers the fundamental role of leaders in sustainable cultures and the responsibilities of top-level leaders as well as others with influence throughout the organization. Chapter 3 examines how the unique identities of sustainable companies form and become the foundations upon which the other aspects of their cultures rest. And finally, in Chapter 4, I examine the critical role of trust in enabling sustainable cultures to thrive.

Part 1

Fundamentals

1 Becoming a sustainable company

Making the case

Chapter purpose

While participating in a business development program with other business owners some time ago, I heard us all stating the same goal for our varied businesses. We wanted to ensure that our companies were ready to grow and succeed for the long term. Several of us described our purpose by explaining what we sell, and we defined success as growth and financial achievements.

I was haunted by the narrowness of this vision. Upon further reflection and research, I've come to believe that corporate purpose and success in the 21st century must mean more than just the products and services we sell and how much money we make. Our employees and customers, as well as others who are interested in our businesses, want to know who we are and what we stand for both as leaders and as companies. Increasingly, the public expects us to contribute to the welfare of society as we pursue profits.

The purpose of this chapter is to show why all companies should become sustainable, a term I use to describe those that have integrated a contribution to society into the core of their business and that perform across four dimensions: Environmental, social, financial, and governance. The chapter introduces the topics that I cover in greater detail throughout the book. It includes an overview of why a company should care about sustainability, defined as its ability to sustain competitive advantage over the long term through strong financial performance, and the integration of environmental, social, and governance factors into the core of the company's strategy and operations. The chapter includes a profile of sustainable companies and the qualities that differentiate them from others.

What is a sustainable company?

The meaning of the expression *sustainable company* in my research and throughout this book is very specific. I use the expression to refer to companies that sustain competitive advantage for the long term by integrating a contribution to society into their business models. These companies show strong performance in the following areas: Financial, environmental, social, and governance.

Committing to a purpose beyond profits is often a first step towards becoming sustainable.[1] Many times purpose-driven companies have integrated social impact into their business models and strategies and have become sustainable as a result.

Companies demonstrate their commitments to the welfare of society in various ways, some through philanthropy and volunteerism, others by striving to do less harm and still others by seeking to do more good. A few have become certified B Corps, defined by the certifying organization B Labs as: "businesses that meet the highest standards of verified social and environmental performance, public transparency, and legal accountability to balance profit and purpose."[2] Throughout this book I reserve the term *sustainable company* to those that meet a very high standard in their financial, environmental, and social performance by integrating sustainability into the core of their businesses.

Why care about becoming a sustainable company?

As business leaders, we have reasons for caring about how our companies affect our world. Certainly, we desire profits. At the same time, many of us also want to contribute to the greater good of society. Indeed, our ability to balance profits with a greater purpose is likely to influence our companies' survival over the long term.

Shift in context

The average tenure of companies on the S&P 500 is dropping steadily. Some are bought, some merge with others, and some go out of business completely. Publicly traded firms die off at the same rate regardless of their age or economic sector; from any point in time a typical company lasts only about ten additional years.[3] The average tenure of S&P 500 companies is dropping steadily from 33 years in 1964 to 24 years in 2016. Analysts predict that by 2027 the average tenure will have dropped to only 12 years.[4]

In a business world increasingly challenged by bio–engineering, robotics, 3-D printing, artificial intelligence, geo–political upheavals, and climate change, our companies must be resilient, or they could be gone tomorrow no matter how successful they appear today. Evidence points to the importance of balancing the pursuit of profits with the commitment to a broader purpose as central to company survival. In fact, Larry Fink, the chairman and chief executive officer of Blackrock, the global investment firm, wrote the following in his 2017 annual letter to CEOs:

> Society is demanding that companies, both public and private, serve a social purpose. To prosper over time, every company must not only deliver financial performance, but also show how it makes a positive contribution to society. Companies must benefit all their stakeholders, including shareholders, employees, customers, and the communities in which they operate.[5]

Stakeholder expectations

Certainly, our shareholders expect us to provide them with healthy returns. However, many others with an interest in our companies, commonly referred to as stakeholders, expect us to consider more than maximizing our profits at all costs. Current and future employees, owners and investors, suppliers, customers, and communities join a long list of critical stakeholders. Unquestionably, the importance of each stakeholder to the success of our businesses varies. Nevertheless, most of us face the rising expectations of stakeholders significant to our companies' success. I cover stakeholder expectations in greater detail in Chapter 6. However, the examples below provide a quick look at what the research is showing concerning the expectations of various stakeholders of importance to many companies.

Millennial employees

People in the workforce expect more of our companies than ever before, no matter what age group they represent. However, millennials' expectations are particularly significant because they now comprise the largest demographic in the labor force. And they want companies to drive change in the world. The 2018 Deloitte Millennial Survey reveals a striking gap between what millennials think companies should achieve and how they view companies' current priorities. They think that companies should address the concerns of a variety of stakeholders while they believe that companies only prioritize profits. Some key points from the millennial survey include:

- 75 percent said that businesses are pursuing their own agendas rather than contributing to the betterment of society.
- 66 percent believe that businesses are only concerned about making money.
- 40 percent hold the opinion that businesses are having a negative impact on the world.[6]

Consumers and communities

Consumers of all ages are interested in businesses addressing the challenges in the communities where they operate. A multinational survey conducted in 2017 found that 77 percent of the participants preferred to purchase from companies with a demonstrated record of showing responsibility to the community. In addition, these consumers were willing to pay 5 to 10 percent more for the products and services offered by these companies.[7]

Investors

Investors care more about our record with sustainability than we think according to a 2016 study conducted by the *MIT Sloan Management Review* in collaboration with the Boston Consulting Group. They found that investors are using data concerning companies' sustainability records because they have noted the positive relationship between a company's sustainability performance and financial performance. When asked why companies' sustainability performance was important to them, they cited many reasons including the creation of long-term value, improved revenue potential, enhanced operational efficiency, and minimized risks.[8]

Clearly our stakeholders – and we all have many – want us to pursue a purpose beyond profits. They want us to recognize the impact that our companies can have on society, and they want us to do something about it. They wish to know whether they can trust us to consider their interests as well as our own. I discuss internal stakeholders, or employees, in greater detail in Chapter 5 and external stakeholders in Chapter 6.

Company performance

In addition to meeting the expectations of stakeholders, companies that address their societal impact perform better, according to Harvard Business School professors, Robert Eccles and George Serafeim. Their results showed how environmental, social, and governance (ESG) performance connects with financial outcomes and transformation. They concluded that for companies "to endure, their strategies must address the interests of all stakeholders; investors, employees, customers, governments, NGOs, and society at large."[9]

Similarly, a 2016 global survey by EY Beacon Institute with Harvard Business Review Analytic Services showed that a commitment to purpose is related to performance outcomes. They found that when purpose guided corporate strategy and decision-making, executives were more able to innovate, successfully engage in ongoing transformation, and deliver revenue growth. The report states that "those companies able to harness the power of purpose to drive performance and profitability enjoy a distinct competitive advantage."[10]

Book premises

This book is based on two premises:

1   Sustainable companies seeking a balance between pursing profits and making a positive contribution to society increase their chances of surviving for the long term. Shifts in context, changing stakeholder expectations, and company performance support this first premise.
2   The second and more fundamental premise of the book is that sustainable companies have cultural profiles that distinguish them from others. The distinctive qualities that they demonstrate fall into the following categories: How leaders think and perform, how the companies view their identities, the degree to which the companies intentionally foster trust, the nature of

their internal culture, how they relate to externals, and how they approach change. The qualities, approaches, and behaviors that comprise this profile are critical for sustainable companies and are desirable for all organizations that want to thrive for the long term.

Why care about culture?

Organizational culture can be difficult to pin down. We feel it and experience it, yet we find it hard to explain. However, a lack of clear definition doesn't stop us from using the term quite frequently. Recently, a colleague told me that although he refers to culture from time to time, it is a murky concept with no practical value. I do not agree with my associate. I believe that organizational culture is a well-researched reality and that understanding it and attending to it is vital to our ability to lead. Culture, as opposed to a fuzzy abstraction, includes what we stand for, how we act, what we encourage, and what we reward. Only by breaking it down into concrete qualities can we understand how it either serves our companies well or hinders our companies' functioning. Organizational culture matters. Our company cultures can contribute to business success, the personal well-being of our people, and the health of our society. On the other hand, organizational culture can also cause great harm.

The perils of toxic cultures

Some organizational cultures are deadly. Too many companies have a crippling work environment where people tolerate bad behavior and disrespect each other. When work is mind-numbing and employees are treated unfairly, businesses can suffer through:

- Drops in productivity.
- Deterioration of employee well-being.
- Reputational damage.

Over the past few years many companies with toxic cultures have suffered financial as well as brand damage due to very public misdeeds. In addition, cultures that encourage chasing profits at any cost can do enormous damage to society. These companies fail their employees, customers, communities, and investors. Let's consider some examples.

Examples of toxic cultures

Uber, the transportation and food delivery company, received a dramatic blow to its image in 2017 from devastating negative publicity. Their long history of complaints from women and others who felt mistreated by their practices came to light. Many issues from passenger safety to workplace discrimination emerged as alarming.

Likewise, Fox News, ESPN, and Ford Motor Company, among many others, came under the public microscope for predatory and sexist cultures. Volkswagen experienced reputation and financial damage from flagrant neglect and reporting fraud related to its environmental sustainability. Wells Fargo encountered the harm of government fines, divestitures by major clients, lawsuits, and brand devaluation from the revelation of widespread fraudulent behaviors.

News of negative cultures is not hard to find. Stories of companies where egregious behaviors were condoned if not encouraged crop up all too often. When the truth of how these companies operate is revealed their reputations take a hard hit. No matter company size or strategy, reputation-related risks are real and can have a devastating impact on the companies' fortunes. Toxic organizational cultures harm employees and society in general. And toxic cultures can threaten a company's survival.

The power of positive cultures

Whereas some cultures are damaging, others are beneficial for:

- Supporting strong business outcomes.
- Promoting the well-being of people who work in the company.
- Contributing to the betterment of society.

Although I explore each of these themes in greater detail in later chapters, I want to present a preview in this chapter.

Culture can support business outcomes

Many factors account for the relationship between positive cultures and strong business performance. Three of the most significant are:

1   Talent attraction.
2   Increased productivity.
3   Greater customer loyalty.

Companies with positive cultures that include a commitment to a purpose beyond profits *attract talent*. People want to work for companies that stand for more than merely creating wealth for shareholders. Therefore, sustainable cultures can enable companies to acquire and retain top-notch employees. In his introduction to the 2017 Gallup report on the *State of the American Workplace*, Chairman and CEO Jim Clifton recommended that companies "Change from a culture of paycheck to a culture of 'purpose'." Clearly supporting his statement,[11] the results of the study show that people choose to work for companies where they can engage in meaningful work. Likewise, they want to be associated with organizations that value employees and treat them with respect.

New entrants to the workforce look for employers that share their values. The *2016 Deloitte Millennial Study* reported on factors influencing employment decisions. Sixty-four percent of the millennials mentioned their personal values and 57 percent said that being true to the organization's overall purpose influenced their decisions. They said they would like for their organizations to focus on a sense of purpose around people rather than growth or profit maximization.[12] I explore this theme in greater detail in Chapter 5.

We all want to be proud of our work and our companies. Think about it. Aren't you more likely to take pride in working for a company that seeks solutions to water shortages in communities where they are located rather than one that pollutes their streams? Of course, work-related motivations vary. Nevertheless, when Facebook surveyed their workforce recently, hearing from thousands, they found that their employees want three things: Career, community, and cause. They value a workplace characterized by respect, trust, and a sense of belonging. They want to be able to use their strengths and desire opportunities for learning and career development. And they want to make an impact on society through their work. To take pride in their workplace, they must believe that the company is doing some good in the world.[13]

We have all heard about how companies such as Google and Salesforce attract talent because of their fun cultures. However, many smaller companies hold their own in the competition for employees because of their cultures. For example, Facilities Management Services (FMS), a relatively small janitorial and cleaning company headquartered in Louisville, Kentucky, attracts and retains employees at a rate far better than the industry average, which in turn gives them the business advantage needed for profitability. They attribute their success to their mission-driven culture. While they care about their financial outcomes, they consider the good that they do for their employees and for the community to be equally important. They claim that "even our reputation is spotless." And customers are drawn to them as a result. Their CEO, Scott Koloms, said, "Our success has been, and always will be, based on one fundamental principle: we care. We care about the people we work with, we care about the communities where we live, and we care about our world."[14]

Positive cultures impact *productivity* most likely due to higher levels of employee engagement. The research that I explore in Chapter 5 shows a clear relationship between employee engagement and other positive characteristics of culture such as trust and feeling valued. And companies with higher levels of employee engagement are more productive. The Gallup organization's work shows that companies with high levels of engagement showed:

- 17 percent more productivity.
- 70 percent reduction in safety incidents.
- 41 percent lower absenteeism.
- 20 percent higher sales.
- 21 percent higher profitability.[15]

Positive cultures generate *customer loyalty*. Increasingly, customers want to patronize companies that share their values. Consider your own choices. Do you want to buy an automobile from a company known for lying about how it affects the environment or a company committed to reducing carbon emissions? And if you have a choice between purchasing your workout gear from a company known for exploiting child labor or another company famous for its fair trade, ethical labor practices, and natural and recycled fabrics, which would you choose? Some of us don't know or care about the ethics of the companies from which we purchase our cars and our clothes. However, an increasing number of us do care about the underlying principles of the companies we patronize. As I mentioned previously, a recent study indicated that over three-fourths of consumers prefer to buy from companies that they view as being responsible to their communities.[16] I go into greater detail on this topic in Chapter 6.

Positive cultures affect employee well-being

Engagement with work and the workplace is related to employees' well-being. The Gallup organization has been studying employee engagement for many years. Recently they reported that American workers who are "actively dis-engaged" – emotionally disconnected from their work and workplace – rate their lives more poorly than do unemployed persons. At the other end of the spectrum are thriving "engaged" employees – American workers enthusiastically involved in their work. In their book on well-being, Tom Rath and Jim Harter, both associated with the Gallup organization, revealed that actively disengaged employees are twice as likely to be diagnosed with depression over the next year as are those who are engaged in their work. Clearly engagement is closely connected with our sense of well-being.[17]

Positive cultures enable company contribution to society

Our own decade-long research program shows that companies producing the best sustainability results, both social and environmental, have more positive cultures than others, as defined by characteristics that fall into the following categories: Leadership, identity, trust, internal culture, external relationships, change capabilities. In the next section I will present a profile of a sustainable company and will describe the qualities that differentiate it from others.

Profile of a sustainable company

Back in 2012, my research colleagues, Bob Eccles and George Serafeim, and I conducted a study focused on companies in the Dow Jones Sustainability Index (DJSI), a family of indices focused exclusively on sustainability and connected with the S&P Dow Jones Indices. We compared sustainable companies, those in the top 20 percent of the Dow Jones Sustainability Index, with traditional companies, those in the bottom 20 percent. The two primary questions that we addressed were:

1   What do sustainable companies do that other companies do not?
2   How do sustainable companies change to support implementation of broad-scale sustainable strategies?

By addressing these questions, we developed a roadmap for others to follow to become sustainable. We described our conclusions in the article "How to Become a Sustainable Company," in the *MIT Sloan Management Review* in 2012.[18] My subsequent research has enabled me to add detail in answering the questions.

What sustainable companies do that others do not

This chapter addresses the first question: What sustainable companies do that other companies do not. I address the second question towards the end of the book after a review of the evidence in the earlier chapters.

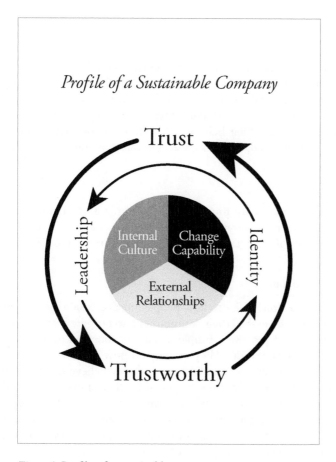

Figure 1 Profile of a sustainable company

Through our research, we found many answers to the first question. The big picture that emerged from our work is illustrated in Figure 1, Profile of a sustainable company. Three of the profile components, leadership, identity, and trust, create the foundation for the other three components, internal organizational culture, external relationships, and change capability.

Sustainable companies demonstrate qualities that differentiate them from others in each of the six profile components described below, as well as a seventh that has emerged from our more recent work: mental models.

Leadership

Leaders in sustainable companies frame or reframe the company identity. They communicate a clear and inspiring vision bolstered by a strong business case. They demonstrate their personal commitment to the vision by taking a long-term view and integrating sustainability into their decision-making. They tolerate moderate risks. I explore leadership in sustainable companies in greater depth in Chapter 2.

Identity

A company's identity includes how they view themselves on the inside as well as how they wish others on the outside to regard them. Sustainable companies tend to think about the world and their place in it differently from others. As a result, they frame or reframe their identity to include their relationship to society at large. Their values and ethics guide their behaviors and they are committed to doing less harm and doing more good. I discuss these concepts more fully in Chapter 3.

Trust

Sustainable companies make trust foundational to their culture. They work to establish trust across their organizations internally. Likewise, they strive to be trustworthy in the eyes of their stakeholders. I will examine trust in Chapter 4.

Internal organizational culture

Internal organizational culture refers to how people function inside their companies. Sustainable companies embed their commitments to purpose beyond profits into policies, systems, and processes. Employees are encouraged to learn from others external to the organization. They understand how their work connects to the company's purpose-driven commitments and they believe that the company values their contribution. They are rewarded for their impact through the company performance management and compensation systems. They believe that sustainability is critical to the long-term health of their companies and thus they are engaged in what they view as meaningful work. I examine internal organizational culture in greater detail in Chapter 5.

External relationships

Sustainable companies interact more with external stakeholders and send clear and consistent messages to them about their purpose, vision, and commitments to sustainability. They care about their reputation with the public and work to become trustworthy. They are more collaborative with externals and they are more likely than others to encourage their suppliers to commit to sustainability.

Change capability

Sustainable companies have stronger track records for both large-scale change and smaller, incremental change. They acknowledge the need for resilience and they work to become change-adept. They make time for and reward continuous learning. People are encouraged to learn by interacting with people external to the organization as well as by taking the time to reflect and learn on the job. Employees are expected to challenge the status quo. They integrate sustainable change with innovation. In Chapter 7 I explore what comprises change capability in greater detail.

Mental models

Sustainable companies' mental models differ from others. Mental models are thinking frameworks through which we interpret our world. They influence our judgments, decisions, and how we approach our work. Sustainable companies tend to hold an outside-in thinking framework which means that, while they strive to do less harm in the world, they also focus on doing more good. They identify the societal challenges or needs that they might address and then assess how to use their capabilities and resources to do so. The mental models of sustainable companies tend to be less rigid than most. People in these companies are aware of the assumptions and biases that underlie their judgments and decisions and are more willing than others to modify their views. I discuss mental models and how they affect a company's ability to change in more detail in Chapter 8.

The chart in Figure 2 summarizes these qualities that differentiate sustainable companies from others.

Example of a sustainable company: Unilever

Unilever, the Dutch–British transnational consumer products company, has made innovation and corporate citizenship central to the way they function. Their culture, including the values that they profess, the behaviors that they encourage, and the decisions that they make, align with their commitments. They have been innovating to address global challenges for many years. As of August 2018, the Unilever website described their Unilever Sustainable Living Plan, launched in 2010, as follows:

A Sustainable Company Is More Likely To Demonstrate These Qualities

Leadership	Inspiring vision of purpose Business case for sustainability Personal commitment to vision Long-term view Tolerate risk Aligned decision-making
Identity	Purpose beyond profit Contribution to society Emphasis on Values and Ethics Do no harm Do more good
Trust	Build trust internally Emphasize trustworthiness externally
Internal Culture	Embed commitments Learn from externals Connect work to purpose Value and reward employees Importance of sustainability to company High engagement
External Relationships	Care about reputation Clear messages Collaborative Encourage sustainability in supply chain
Change Capability	Strong change track record Continuous learning Resilience No status quo thinking Integrate innovation
Mental Models	Outside in thinking Aware of assumptions and biases Open to change

Figure 2 A sustainable company is more likely to demonstrate these qualities

- Assist a billion people improve their health and well-being.
- Cut their environmental impact in half.
- Enhance the livelihoods of people in their supply chain.

In describing how they treat employees, they emphasize understanding people as individuals. They equip their employees to adopt an owner's mindset through collaboration, continuous learning, clarity of purpose, and financial rewards.[19] Their revenue in 2010 of 46.3 billion euros grew to 53.7 billion euros by 2017; another indication that the platform of people, planet, and profits can dynamically reinforce each other. And in 2017 its Sustainable Living Brands "grew 46% faster than the rest of the business and delivered 70% of Unilever's turnover growth."[20]

Summary and conclusions

Over the past decade the context for doing business has shifted dramatically. Our stakeholders expect more of our companies. They expect us to make a positive contribution to society while we earn. In other words, they want us to become sustainable. Our stakeholders have access to more information about us than ever through social media. As we respond to their expectations, our company performance often improves.

Organizational culture plays a powerful role in our outcomes as we strive to be sustainable. Toxic cultures can lead to our demise while positive cultures can support our ongoing success. I refer to these positive cultures as sustainable cultures. They support positive business outcomes, promote the well-being of people who work in our companies, and contribute to the betterment of society. The components of these sustainable cultures include leadership, identity, trust and trustworthiness, internal culture, external culture, and change capacity including modifiable mental models. Our research shows that the cultures of sustainable companies are unique. And while these cultures are critical for their success, they are applicable to all companies.

Your turn: initial assessment

Before we examine the characteristics of organizational culture in greater detail, I suggest that you describe your culture as you see it currently. I recommend that you consider both your company overall, and any parts of the company that you can influence. Some of you may be able to influence the entire company, for example if you are the CEO or a senior leader. Others of you may have more limited influence over parts of the company. Begin by assessing your company overall. Then complete the assessment again for the part of the company where you have the most influence.

Part 1: what does your company stand for?

Describe what you believe to be the basic purpose and values of your company. In other words, what does your company stand for? And how would the public describe it? Don't read this off your company website. Think about your own experiences within the company and what a magazine article might say about your company after interviewing a cross-section of employees and other stakeholders.

In addition to making a profit, our company's purpose is:	The company values include:

Part 2: describe your area of influence

Consider the part of your company where you have influence (I will refer to this as your area of influence throughout the book). Describe it based on your own experiences and how you believe others view it.

My area(s) of influence:	
Our (my) purpose is:	Our (my) values include:

Tool: how to do a quick check on culture

You have just described your culture based on your own perceptions. You can gather some information to test your own impressions without taking the time and effort to carry out a thorough culture assessment. Here are some suggestions:

- Ask a few of your peers to describe the culture and values of the company.
- Ask some people outside of your company to describe the culture. You might ask some friends, family, or others in your network.
- Look at what people are saying about your company on social media. You can do a Google search as a first step. You might also consider looking at some websites where employees review their companies such as Glassdoor, or JobAdvisor, or RateMyEmployer. You may find your company in these reviews.

Notes

1 Sakis Kotsantonis and George Serafeim, kks advisors, personal communication, February 20, 2018. Refers to definitions of a purpose-driven and sustainable company.

2 B Lab website accessed on September 18, 2018: https://bcorporation.net/about-b-corps.

3 "How Long Do Firms Live?" *Science Daily*, Santa Fe Institute, April 2015. Available at: www.sciencedaily.com/releases/2015/04/150401132856.htm.

4 Scott D. Anthony, S. Patrick Viguerie, Evan I. Schwartz, and John Van Landeghem, "Corporate Longevity Forecast: Creative Destruction is Accelerating," *Innosight*, February 2018. Available at: www.innosight.com/wp-content/uploads/2017/11/Innosight-Corporate-Longevity-2018.pdf.

5 *Larry Fink's Annual Letter to CEOs: A Sense of Purpose.* Website accessed September 20, 2018. Available at: https://seekingalpha.com/article/4137819-larry-finks-2018-letter-ceos-sense-purpose.

6 Michele Parmelee, "Uneasy, Pessimistic and Concerned: Insights from the 2018 Deloitte Millennial Survey," *Deloitte Insights*, 2018. Available at: www2.deloitte.com/global/en/pages/about-deloitte/articles/millennialsurvey.html.

7 *In Good Company: The Value of Conscious Consumers*, A Union+Weber Research Report, (Zendesk, 2017) accessed on September 9, 2018. Available at: https://zen-marketing-content.s3.amazonaws.com/content/whitepapers/Conscious%20Consumerism.pdf.

8 Gregory Unruh, David Kiroon, Nina Kruschwitz, Martin Reeves, Holger Rubel, and Alexander Meyer Zumfelde, "Investing for a Sustainable Future," *MIT Sloan Management Review Research Report*, May 11, 2016. Website accessed September 21, 2018. Available at: http://marketing.mitsmr.com/offers/SU2016/57480-MITSMR-BCG-Sustainability2016.pdf?cid=1.

9 Robert Eccles and George Serafeim, "The Performance Frontier," *Harvard Business Review*, May 2013. Reprint r1305B.

10 "The Business Case for Purpose," *Harvard Business Review: A Harvard Business Review Analytic Services Report* sponsored by EY, 2016, 2.

11 *Gallup State of the American Workplace*, Gallup Inc., 2017, 3. Available at: www.gallup.com/workplace/238085/state-american-workplace-report-2017.aspx.

12 *2016 Deloitte Millennial Survey: Winning Over the Next Generation of Leaders*, Deloitte, 2016. Available at: www2.deloitte.com/content/dam/Deloitte/global/Documents/About-Deloitte/gx-millenial-survey-2016-exec-summary.pdf.

13 Lori Golar, Janell Gale, Bryn Harrington, and Adam Grant, "The Three Things Employees Really Want: Career, Community and Cause," *Harvard Business Review*, February 20, 2018. Available at: https://hbr.org/2018/02/people-want-3-things-from-work-but-most-companies-are-built-around-only-one.

14 Scott Koloms, President, FMS, personal conversation with author, March 6, 2018.

15 *State of the American Workplace*, Gallup Organization, 2017. Available at: https://news.gallup.com/reports/178514/state-american-workplace.aspx.

16 *In Good Company: The Value of Conscious Consumers*, A Union+Weber Research Report, (Zendesk: 2017), accessed on September 9, 2018. Available at: https://zen-marketing-content.s3.amazonaws.com/content/whitepapers/Conscious%20Consumerism.pdf.

17 Tom Rath and Jim Harter, *Well-Being: The Five Essential Elements*, (Gallup Press, 2010).

18 Robert Eccles, Kathleen Miller Perkins, and George Serafeim, "How to Become a Sustainable Company," *MIT Sloan Management Review*, Summer 2012, 53, no. 4, 43–50.
19 Developing and Engaging our People. Unilever website accessed September 15, 2018. Available at: www.unilever.com/sustainable-living/our-strategy/embedding-sustainability/developing-and-engaging-our-people.
20 "Unilever's Sustainable Living Brands Deliver 70% of Turnover Growth in 2017," *Sustainable Brands*, Business Case, May 10, 2018, accessed September 24, 2018. Available at: www.sustainablebrands.com/news_and_views/business_case/sustainable_brands/unilevers_sustainable_living_brands_delivered_70_tur.

2   Leadership in sustainable companies
Character and values

Chapter purpose

As Ray Kroc once said, "The quality of leaders is reflected in the standards they set for themselves."[1] High standards are essential for leaders of sustainable companies. They have a weighty responsibility. Those at the top have the power to frame or reframe the company identity, including purpose and values. And they are responsible for creating an inspiring vision based on that identity. Nevertheless, they can't realize the vision on their own. They need the assistance of leaders throughout the organization who can make the vision come alive in their own areas. Therefore, all of us can lead these efforts, regardless of our roles.

The purpose of this chapter is to explore leadership in sustainable companies. The chapter examines the roles of top-level leaders and explores how all employees can lead from wherever they are in the organization. Everyone has a role to play in creating a sustainable culture. This chapter does not provide an inventory of leadership skills to develop. Instead of focusing on what a leader should do, this chapter concentrates on how a leader should be.

Importance of character and values

I believe that everyone can lead an organization towards purpose beyond profits, even without a formal position of authority. The trick is to allow our heartfelt purpose to guide our performance no matter what our job title. Only upon finding the meaning in our own work can we influence others to do the same. People are attracted to others who are authentic and competent and live by clear values and purpose. Our employees, customers, and other interested parties, often referred to as stakeholders, watch for evidence that our company purpose is genuine. So too do they look for a reason to believe in leaders based on perceptions of their authenticity and consistency in words and deeds.

Leaders of sustainable companies influence others by who they are. While it is easy to find research on leadership styles and skills, it is much harder to find work on leadership character. Yet I believe that our ability to handle the complex challenges that we face today in our global economy hinges on the moral fiber of leadership.

My research shows that leadership character is critically important in organizations. To illustrate this point, I present a quote offered by an employee of a socially responsible business:

I've worked with many leaders I did not respect because they took credit from their teams, were overly hungry for power, knew far less than they led others to believe and did not truly care for or invest in their people. This management team is the complete opposite. I have the utmost respect for each person on our management team and cherish the moments I get to work alongside them because I feel it makes me a better professional and a better person.[2]

Wouldn't all of us like for our employees to describe us similarly? When my research team asks employees to tell us what they look for in a leader, rather than listing skills they talk about their desire for leaders who are honest, ethical, and courageous. They look for leaders who care about them.

Unfortunately, on our global stage, leaders with character seem to be in short supply. Nevertheless, I continue to believe that character counts. Character has become increasingly important for leadership in a world short on trust and for those seeking a path towards a better future.

Leaders at the top

While all leaders shape culture in a variety of ways, those at the top have the unique responsibility of setting the direction and purpose for the company. Leaders at the top of sustainable companies must communicate and live by an inspiring vision. According to Rob Frederick, Vice President and Director of Corporate Responsibility at Brown–Forman, one of the leading producers and distributors of premium alcoholic beverages in the world, "Because companies tend to be siloed, implementation of sustainability strategies takes a leader who can see and communicate across the organization and put the various pieces of the sustainability puzzle together."[3] From their broad organizational perspective, top-level leaders can engage the various constituents in developing a shared vision that comes alive for everyone in all parts of the organization.

Understanding current state

Before they can organize the puzzle, top-level leaders must first understand how others in the organization view the pieces. And perceptions vary. My company has been in the business of assessing organizational culture for a long time. Over the years, we have consistently found a disconnect between leaders' and employees' views of the culture. These differences surprise leaders. One of our clients told me that through an organizational culture assessment, he learned that there were many cultures – not just one – in his company. He was shocked by what he considered to be lack of alignment. To effectively communicate and lead the organization to *what can be*, leaders must first understand *what is*.

Understanding perceptions of the culture

Assessments of culture, no matter how conducted, almost always show that top-level leaders believe trust and engagement are stronger in the company than their employees' responses indicate. Similarly, top-level leaders believe in the strength of the company's track record with change to a greater degree than do their employees. They are more likely than their employees to think that the public views the company as ethical, and they evaluate their messages concerning company purpose and commitments more positively. Leaders' beliefs that their employees feel valued are stronger than employees' actual perceptions warrant. In fact, positive perceptions of company culture tend to deteriorate with each level down from executives. Leaders must have a clear view of their starting point before they can steer the culture to a more sustainable condition.

Understanding of the vision

Top-level leaders are in a unique position to set direction around purpose and to craft a vision. However, our research shows that often they are unaware of how employees perceive their visions. Leaders often rate the clarity of their vision and their ability to inspire others higher than do their employees. Likewise, employees' understandings of the company's values are less clear than leaders believe. And while leaders say that they integrate their commitments to purpose into their decision-making, often employees are skeptical.

Differences catch leaders by surprise

Most leaders are shocked by the discrepancies between their own perceptions and their employees' experiences. They are especially surprised by their employees' lack of awareness and understanding of the vision and how they, the leaders, are guided by it. We find these differences between top-level leaders and employees across the board in companies in every industry, whether large or small. While not as serious, the disconnects show up even in companies that define themselves as socially responsible.

We have come up with plenty of explanations for the discrepancies. Sometimes the culture within the senior ranks does indeed differ from the rest of the organization. For example, the systems that support culture, such as rewards and compensation, are often unique for higher-level leaders. In other cases, employees bring only good news to the attention of their managers and senior leaders. And sometimes senior leaders are mistaken about what their mid-level managers are communicating to their employees.

We have reached the tentative conclusion that either the leaders have not communicated their commitments clearly, or their companies have not actually incorporated the vision into the core business. If they had embedded their sustainability strategies into all their most critical processes their employees would certainly be more aware of their importance. To make the vision real, leaders must communicate it clearly, demonstrate how it influences their behavior, and embed the vision into the core of the organization and its operations.

No matter what the causes of the inconsistencies in perceptions, leaders at every level will benefit from understanding and addressing any discrepancies that they find. If leaders want people to buy in to a company vision and internalize it, they must take steps to appreciate the various perspectives. People will commit only when trust is widespread, they understand the vision, are inspired by it, and believe that it is real. They want to see their top-level leaders live by it.

In the most sustainable companies, employees believe that a commitment to sustainability is critical to the long-term success of the company. This conviction comes from the leaders' business case for the commitments and strategies, and the degree to which they have embedded purpose and values into the functioning of the organization. For example, employees look for whether top-level leaders are willing to take a long-term view for the sake of finding solutions to complex problems. They look for evidence that leaders have incorporated their commitments into their decision-making. They evaluate whether their leaders are prepared to take some risks in search of these solutions. All of these factors influence whether employees will internalize the vision and work to make it real.

Once committed to the vision, people throughout the company want to contribute to moving it forward. When employees understand how their own work connects with the vision they are more likely to engage with it. Thus, leaders must ensure that the processes are in place to enable the employees to understand these connections.

When engagement is high, people are more productive and loyal. As a result, the company can more effectively pursue its purpose. Setting the direction and guiding people towards trust, purpose, and engagement are perhaps the most critical responsibilities of top-level leaders. To convey the vision, leaders should tell compelling stories.

Case: changing a culture through stories

Recently we worked with an organization that I will refer to as The Urban Company. When a new leader joined the organization, morale was low. Since I was aware of the turmoil, I was not surprised that many felt unappreciated and burned out. This new leader was determined to steer the organization towards a renewed culture with a vision that would inspire people and lift the malaise. Soon after he arrived, he gathered the employees together in a town hall where he spoke to them from his heart through vivid and personal stories. He started by telling a story about his life. He described a time-line of critical events over the course of his career including helping evacuate a high-rise in 90-degrees-plus temperatures during the New York City blackout of 2003. He talked about how he felt when leading people through the national tragedy of 9/11 as well as through super-storm Sandy. He ended this part of his presentation by claiming that he considered his work to be a calling – not just a job. And he challenged the employees to reconsider how they viewed their own work.

He built on his story by recognizing what the organization had accomplished over the recent past. He thanked people personally for their own individual contributions. Then he moved to his vision for the future of the organization. He stated, "I will give my time, energy and commitment to helping us become a world-class organization. I honestly believe that we can become a best in class standard against which other similar organizations can measure themselves."

He promised to respect the organization's history by repeating a maxim from Midwest cattle country, "Don't tear down the fence until you know why it was put there in the first place." He ended by describing his values and declaring that values count. This new leader understood the power of an inspiring vision illustrated with compelling stories. His town hall speech set the stage for a new era in the organization.

Leaders at all levels: formal and informal

All of us can influence others whether we are a CEO, a senior leader, a mid-level manager, team leader, or informal trailblazer without a formal title of authority. Our ability to influence others defines us as leaders regardless of our titles. Leadership sage John Maxwell has argued for years that the number one myth about leadership is that it comes from having a formal position or title. Maxwell asserts that leadership is no more or less than the ability to influence others. Moreover, he argues that holding a formal position of power does not automatically make one a leader. Any one of us with the ability to influence is a leader and can make the organization better.[4]

Sources of influence

A leader's influence can come from a variety of sources. Each of us can influence others if we draw on one or more of the sources of power available to us.

Legitimate: power of position

When leaders are in formal positions of leadership at the top of the organization, they wield the power that goes with it. These top-level leaders such as CEOs and senior managers do have the authority to set direction and make the rules. Depending on how their position of authority is defined, they are very likely to have the power to make final decisions about many things. And, to the degree that people in the organization respect their positions, they derive power from their job titles.

Coercive: power to punish

People who are in formal positions of authority usually can determine what gets punished in the organization. Although sometimes people who do not hold formal positions of authority still have the power to punish. For example, informal leaders can punish others by withholding information or approval from them. Leaders can coerce behaviors with any kind of threat available to them.

Reward: power to reward

Formal leaders generally can reward others through praise, promotions, or money. Although, as with coercive power, people who lack formal leadership positions may still have reward power. For example, people can reward others by sharing information, including them on teams, and praising them for attitudes and behaviors.

Expert: power of knowledge and skill

When people have knowledge or skill that others value, they hold expert power. Expert power is especially potent if this expertise is unique or scarce. For example, researchers who know how to derive value from "big data" have expert power.

Referent: power of relationships and admiration

Referent power comes from character and is more robust than any other. Referent power is based on respect and relationships. Therefore, leaders who are guided by purpose and values and who have integrity in the eyes of others are likely to hold referent power. They are probably influential, no matter what their formal title.

Which power source works best?

Many times, people have more than one source of power. For example, if you are in a formal authority role that others recognize, you have legitimate power. However, most likely you can reward and punish as well. Despite the overlaps, the strongest base of power is referent, especially when combined with other sources of influence.

The strength of referent power

The picture that emerges of the most influential leaders depicts a person who is believed to be knowledgeable, trustworthy, and competent, and who is liked and respected by others. These people can influence no matter what their position or title in the organization. And, in most cases, those who are in positions of authority yet do not have the respect and goodwill of others, will not remain powerful. Their legitimacy in the eyes of others fades. They may be able to influence behaviors for the short term. However, in the longer term, people will cease following them.

The limitations of legitimate and coercive power

For many years, I have assisted companies with culture and the people-side of change. More than once I have heard top-level leaders say something like the following: "We don't have to worry about how people feel about their work. We pay them to do the job. They will do what we say." I have concluded that either they are ignorant of what makes people tick, are kidding themselves, or don't care about tapping the creativity and passions that enable people to perform at their best. Think about it. When was the last time you gave your all to a task because someone commanded it of you? None of us, no matter what our formal positions, have the power to make others care. We may be able to influence behavior, at least temporarily. However, a carrot and stick approach will not bring out the best in people and influence them for the longer term.

True enough, people often do comply with direct orders. However most of us don't like to work for leaders who merely give orders and expect us to fall into line. This kind of leadership creates resistance where it would not have occurred under other circumstances.

When leaders manage by edict, employees often engage in passive aggressive behaviors. For example, in my own work I have heard people claim that they didn't follow through on an order because they didn't understand what the boss wanted. Others have smiled and acted like they were complying when the boss was looking while doing just the opposite when she turned her back. I have witnessed disgruntled employees lambasting the company when talking with their friends and families. Worse yet, I have run across their criticisms of the company on social media. When leaders rule through command and control, absenteeism and turnover are likely to go up and nothing much gets done. Too often, the people who gave the orders in the first place are unaware of their own roles in the lackluster results of their organizations.

Case: power of purpose and character

As I recall leaders in our client organizations, one stands out. Mark was an hourly employee in an oil refinery where he also served as a union steward. Mark believed in the power of strong collaboration between union and management. He understood that both groups shared common goals. He believed that an organization should enable high performance through people who were competent, valued, and empowered. He held that the plant could carry out its mission, serve its customers, and make a profit only if all employees were inspired to make a difference in their own jobs every day.

People were drawn to Mark because he was smart, personable, and trustworthy. He had the ability to communicate effectively across the organizational boundaries including up and down the hierarchy. While he did not have the formal authority to give orders, nor to reward and punish others for their behaviors, he had significant influence throughout the company. He could persuade managers and peers alike to listen to his ideas and often adopt his recommendations. People looked to see how he reacted to change before determining their own responses.

I worked with Mark on a joint union–management partnership to build a world-class training system for the chemical operators, the first of its kind in this company. The initiative inspired the operators because they welcomed the personal and team growth that the training would bring. As a result, they could make a stronger contribution to the company and to their customers.

Similar initiatives had always been led by managers in the past because of the power of their positions. However, this time the executives tapped Mark to carry the program forward even though he was not in a formal management role. I was not surprised. He was clearly the person with the vision and the ability to inspire others to sign on. His clarity of purpose, along with his ability to communicate a strong business case for it, enabled him to tap the enthusiasm of both management and labor.

No matter where you are in the organization, at the very top, in the middle, or anywhere else, you can lead towards the creation of a positive culture by drawing on your own sources of power.

Who you are and how you view others

To use your sources of power and the influence available to you, start by understanding yourself. Then seek to understand others and your mutual and collective purposes, needs, and goals. Finally, appreciate and value diversity.

Understand yourself

If we do not have a clear understanding of ourselves, our values, motives, strengths, and weaknesses, we will not be effective leaders. Do you have a clear understanding of your own life purpose and where your work fits? Many of us are so busy *doing* that we don't take the time to ask ourselves why. Take the time. As you reflect on your own life with its defining moments, ask yourself what stands out. Identify when you have been at your best and your worst. Ask yourself what has energized you over your life to date and what has been the most distasteful to you and drained your energy. As you reflect, patterns are likely to emerge and point you to values and motivations that have guided your life and the decisions you have made to date. You will note what you have been willing to sacrifice and what you would never give up. You will identify your sources of pride and areas of vulnerability. And as you reflect, your understanding of your own unique life purpose is likely to emerge.

Next, reflect on where work fits into your life. We are a pessimistic society these days. We are concerned and anxious about the future in a world filled with terrorism, vast political divides, income inequality, and climate change. Many, if not most of us want to do our part to find solutions to the many problems that plague our world and we may believe that our work provides us with the best opportunity for making an impact on society.[5]

If we work full-time, we are spending close to a third of our time on the job during our working years. Our work represents a greater proportion of our lives than any other single endeavor. Therefore, many of us want our work to be meaningful, although each of us will have our own ideas of what meaningful work looks like. The question that all of us should ask ourselves is what our work means to us. Unless we are volunteering, we are all working for a paycheck. Yet our pay and perks do not provide us with meaning. Meaning comes from engagement and a sense of purpose. It comes from the conviction that we are contributing to something bigger than ourselves. Ask yourself, what is the meaning of your work? If your only answer is that you work to receive a paycheck, you will never be able to inspire and lead others.

It is easier to find the significance of our work when our companies stand for a purpose beyond profits. Nevertheless, no matter how purpose-driven our companies, to become effective leaders we must understand the meaning of our own work. When we have this deep understanding of our purpose, we can take the next step to becoming a leader of others.

Understand others

Armed with a clear understanding of our own life purpose and how it integrates with our work, our next step is to seek an understanding of others. In his book *The 7 Hidden Reasons Employees Leave*,[6] Leigh Branham lists four fundamental human needs:

- Need for trust.
- Need to have hope.
- Need to feel worthy and respected.
- Need to feel competent.

Effective leaders honor those fundamental needs.

Respect diversity

We don't all think alike and within our differences lies the key to creativity and innovation. I remember a conversation I had with my own team several years ago. We had encountered some rough spots in our work together and were exploring what might be causing the problems and what we might change to alleviate the stress. As we contemplated how each of us viewed our team and working groups in general, I said that I always look for the similarities within a group. Another of my colleagues said that she always looks for the differences among the members. At the time, I viewed her point of view as flawed because I believed that focusing on differences could hide common goals and lead to conflict. I viewed conflict as the precursor to group dysfunction. In retrospect, I understand her perspective in a new way. Her awareness of the power of diversity and her assumption that differences and even conflict could strengthen rather than diminish a group rings true to me now. By listening to understand, I changed my own views of how groups might function best.

Effective leaders at every level seek to understand others by exploring what they believe and how they see the world. They do not make assumptions about others. Rather, they are eager to listen and learn.

Leading from where you are: what you can do

No matter what your position in the organization, you can always contribute to a positive, innovative, and sustainable culture.

Enabling collective conversations

Everyone can enable the collective conversations that lead to a positive culture of trust, caring, and engagement. While the company vision is important, no matter how inspiring it is, it will mean very little unless people throughout the organization can engage with each other to explore what it means to them. Through these collective conversations, people can examine and incorporate diverse points of view that make the vision come alive for them in their own work.

Not long ago, we asked our network of readers and clients to comment on the following two statements:

1   I trust the leaders of my company/organization to consistently do what is right.
2   I trust the leaders of most companies/organizations to consistently do what is right.

The results were revealing. Out of the 52 people who responded, over half (58 percent) disagreed with the first statement and close to half (48 percent) disagreed with the second. Yet, based on my own experience, I have concluded that most of us truly want to do what is right. And all of us want to be trusted. However, if this informal and admittedly unscientific survey is even close to accurate, most of the workforce do not trust leaders to do what is right.

I interpreted this somewhat alarming disconnect to come from a lack of consensus concerning the meanings of "leaders" and "doing what is right" – subjective concepts at best. In a diverse workforce, opinions of who is a leader and what is right will vary. What kind of leader? Right for whom? Right in what context? Who gets to define it? Only through conversations across the organization will anything close to consensus emerge about behaviors that align with the company values and vision and doing what is right.

Yet, I have found that organizations rarely create the space for enterprise-wide airing of all those assorted points of view. Perhaps we fear that debilitating conflict might result. Or maybe we assume that reaching consensus will be too hard and will impede what we consider to be our real work. Very likely, some of us avoid the conversations because we want to impose our own definitions of what is right onto others and really don't care what they think. None of these possible explanations reflects true leadership.

Refusal to recognize diverse points of view will not eliminate their effects on the culture. Trust, the cornerstone of a positive culture, requires unguarded yet respectful inquiry into mixed perspectives on core issues such as purpose, values, vision. When handled well, enterprise-wide conversations will contribute to a positive culture. The airing of various points of view will enable the most creative ideas to emerge.

Open discussions can build greater engagement and stronger commitments to the shared goals of the organization. The conversations will be most effective when the participants have the skills to engage in what can be difficult exchanges. Several of our client companies offer their employees training on the skills they need to participate constructively in these conversations. Often, they also develop protocols that ensure the conversations are productive.

Aligning actions with words

Let's face it, leaders can say anything but if their actions don't back up their words, they will not be trusted. For example, even when leaders at the top present a strong business case for their vision, unless their behaviors are consistent with it, others are unlikely to accept it as real.

I remember my shock the first time we worked with a leader who presented himself and his company as truly committed to a culture of respect and empowerment. However, as we became more familiar with the company, we discovered that the story he told the public differed dramatically from reality. As we got a closer look at how he functioned, we became aware of a major disconnect between what he said the company stood for and how he and others behaved. While they claimed to value the well-being of every employee, they did not move quickly to stop the sexual harassment occurring in the company even when they were clearly aware of it. It took the threat of a union campaign to get their attention. We were not surprised to find that the employees were cynical and distrustful. Corporate spin can do great damage. The visible character of a leader eclipses all claims.

Even in the absence of deliberate corporate spin, inconsistencies between leaders' behaviors and their stated vision and values will depress engagement. Consider the following example. We work with a company whose leaders have clearly committed to acting as a socially responsible business, or so it seems to us. However, an assessment of the company's culture revealed a widespread lack of understanding of the company commitments within several pockets of the organization. Note the statements from employees:

> We have a corporate sustainability goal. But day-to-day activities don't necessarily support that goal. Financial performance trumps everything. Senior management may talk sustainability but the people doing the work do not. I think everyone agrees philosophically – actions may not reflect philosophy and the definitions of sustainability aren't clear.

Evidently, this company's leaders still have work to do to engage the entire organization in their efforts, despite their good intentions and the progress that they have made.

Influencing upwards

In his recent article, "4 Ways Managers Can Exercise Their Agency to Change the World," Harvard Business School professor George Serafeim recommends influencing upwards.[7] He suggests building a strong case that social impact can enhance company performance while also taking a pragmatic approach that enables incremental successes. He argues for establishing lines of communication upwards so that you can use your rational arguments as well as your passion to propose opportunities that can have a social as well as a business impact. Merely making a righteous case for doing good is unlikely to succeed. Preparation and persistence increase the likelihood of influencing upwards.

Summary and conclusions

None of us can build a culture on our own in our organizations. Yet each of us can contribute to it. To lead a sustainable organization, first seek to understand the current culture and what it will take to ensure that it is cohesive and supportive of the company vision. Take the time to reflect and understand yourself and others. Seek out the similarities that unite people in your organization as well as the differences that contribute to creativity and innovation. We all have access to power in one form or another. Identify your source(s) of power, and consider strengthening your referent power. Rely on your entire constellation of powers to influence others in the direction of a purpose beyond profits.

Your turn: leadership assessment

Understand yourself

This reflection exercise is meant to help you clarify your own life purpose and where your work fits.

Reflect on your life

Reflect on the high points and low points of your life to date. What, if any, patterns emerge that guide you towards a life purpose? Jot down your thoughts in the table below.

In the left-hand column, list or describe the high points of your life including your work life. In the right-hand column, reflect on why this was a high point for you. Then do the same for your low points.	
My life's high points: When I felt most alive and happy	**Why this was a high point**

My life's low points: **When I was least happy**	**Why this was a low point**

Note any patterns that emerge from this reflection. What has energized you? What has drained you?

What values and motivations have guided your life to date?

Reflect on your work

The purpose of my work is:

I would like the purpose of my work to be:

If you found a discrepancy between how you view your current work's purpose and what you would like it to be, how might you close this gap?

Understand others

Fundamental human needs

> **When you interact with others, how do you honor their fundamental human needs for trust, hope, respect, and competence?**

Opportunities for collective conversations

> **What are your opportunities for leading collective conversations that respect diversity?**

Notes

1 Ray Kroc quotes. *BrainyQuote.com*, BrainyMedia Inc., 2018, accessed November 1, 2018. Available at: www.brainyquote.com/quotes/ray_kroc_390229.
2 Comment, SCALA survey, August 2018.
3 Personal communication, May 30, 2012.
4 John Maxwell, *Developing the Leader Within You 2.0*, Preface, (HarperCollins, 2018).
5 *The Deloitte Millennial Survey 2018*. Website accessed September 8, 2018. Available at: www2.deloitte.com/global/en/pages/about-deloitte/articles/millennialsurvey.html.
6 Leigh Branhman, *The 7 Hidden Reasons Employees Leave: How to Recognize the Subtle Signs and Act Before it is Too Late*, (AMACOM, Special Edition, 2012).
7 George Serafeim, "4 Ways Managers Can Exercise Their Agency to Change the World," The Palladium Group, website accessed October 24, 2018. Available at: http://thepalladiumgroup.com/research-impact/managers-agency-george-serafeim.

3 Company identity

Purpose, values, and vision

Chapter purpose

How would you describe your company's character? Do you think your description would match how the public views it? As Abraham Lincoln once said, "Character is like a tree and reputation like a shadow. The shadow is what we think of it, the tree is the real thing."[1] A company's character or identity includes how people inside view it and how they present it to the public. All companies have identities, some stronger than others. An organization's internal culture and company reputation are built on its identity. Therefore, identity is the second foundational building block of culture. Identity is closely connected with the first building block, leadership. The previous chapter focused on the character of leaders. This chapter looks at company character. Company identity or character influences everything else in a culture.

The purpose of this chapter is to explore identity. We will examine what it is, why it is so important, how it develops, and how it affects reputation.

What is identity and why is it important?

In psychology we define identity as how people define themselves. Our identity or character includes the values that guide our choices and how we present ourselves to others. Many times, we assume our identity first from our parents and others in our community. However, identity isn't fixed. It evolves over time with experiences, learning, and self-reflection. Our identity can shift as we ask ourselves who we are, who we want to be, and what we truly value.

Company identity defined

Similarly, company identity includes how insiders define the company and how they present it to outsiders. Just as personal identity begins with our relationships with our parents, most often company identity starts with the founders and can evolve over time through experiences and reflection.

Strong versus weak company identities

Sustainable companies tend to have strong identities that guide their decisions and behaviors. They tend to have a strong and powerful sense of who they are as a company. In a *Harvard Business Review* article, Paul Leinwand and Cesare Mainardi describe those with weak identities as merely trying to keep up with the market. They deploy strategies that are so incoherent that no one really understands what the company is about. On the other hand, companies with strong identities are clear about their purpose and can "declare what value they are able to create and for whom."[2]

Purpose values and vision as identity

A company's identity is embodied in its purpose and mission, vision and values. Our research shows that the top leaders' vision, based on the company purpose and values, is critical to becoming a sustainable company. One of my company's business advisors told me that "Companies with purpose don't just sell products and services. They give people a reason to believe." And they communicate that reason through their purpose and mission, vision and values.

Rosabeth Moss Kanter, a widely recognized expert on organizations, maintains that an increasing number of successful companies do give people a reason to believe. They emphasize purpose, values, and long-term institution building. These socially responsible companies believe that they are inherently connected to society at large, and thus have obligations as members of society beyond mere economic transactions. According to Kanter, while financial success is important to them, they embrace it partly if not wholly so that they can carry out their commitments to society.[3]

In their article, *From Corporate Citizenship to Corporate Statesmanship*, authors George Kell, founder of the United Nations Global Compact, and Martin Reeves, senior partner of the Boston Consulting Group, stated, "Businesses need to be deeply embedded in society to positively affect it, and have their activities sanctioned and supported by it. Business leaders can achieve this by placing social value at the heart of their business models."[4] As this quote implies, truly sustainable companies do more than engage in corporate philanthropy as a sideline to their real business. They incorporate social value into their missions, visions, and business models. Sustainable companies believe that they have a responsibility to society at large, not just to their shareholders. Thus, serving society is part of their identity.

Companies often communicate their purpose and mission, or why they exist and what they do, as well as their vision and values, what they desire to become and what they stand for, on their websites. For example, furniture retailer Ikea indicates that the company is in business to make life better for people.[5] They describe how they carry out that purpose through their mission, which they describe as follows: Providing home furnishing products that are functional and affordable.

Household goods company Seventh Generation claims that they aim to inspire a revolution among consumers that nurtures the health of the next seven generations.[6] The Kellogg Company declares that their purpose is "nourishing families so they can flourish and thrive."[7] These statements all describe company purpose as a significant aspect of identity.

Vision and values are also central to identity. Our own personal values are usually fiercely held and resistant to change because they come from our deepest human needs and convictions. They serve as our guiding principles between right and wrong. Our values have an enormous impact on how we think and the judgments that we make. However, we may not talk about our personal values explicitly very often. Rarely if ever do we write them out and hang them up in our homes or include them in our newsy holiday cards to friends.

On the other hand, companies frequently post their collective values on plaques inside the company and on their websites for the public to see. Nevertheless, many declarations of company vision and values are bland and seem to have little impact on how the company functions. In general, employees cannot recite the company vision and values without reading the plaques. In those rare cases where employees can describe the vision and values, very few, if any, can explain how they guide their behaviors. The standard lists of values usually include something about integrity, respect, and honesty. While the stated values can be hollow and meaningless, they tend to play a prominent role in sustainable companies.

Case: Ikea – vision, values and culture

Ikea's website states that their vision is "to create a better life for everyday people." They list several values that they claim inform their culture. Some of the values that they publicize include togetherness, cost-consciousness, caring for people and planet, simplicity, give and take responsibility, lead by example, and daring to be different.[8] And their website offers examples of how these values guide them. For instance, they list simplicity as a value and they claim that it influences their culture which is informal and pragmatic. Glassdoor, the website where current and former employees review companies, seems to confirm their claim. The evaluations include many references to their relaxed and fun culture. Furthermore, Ikea has won several workplace culture awards over the last few years that validate their statements.[9]

- America's Best Employers for Diversity, *Forbes*, 2018.
- The 100 Best Companies to Work for, *Fortune*, 2017.
- Best Places to Work, *Glassdoor*, 2017.
- People's 50 Companies That Care 2017, *People Magazine*, 2017.

Case: Eileen Fisher – purpose in action

American clothing brand Eileen Fisher Inc. clearly communicates company identity by talking about vision, purpose, and values. In a 2015 interview with

Conscious Company Media, Eileen Fisher, the founder of the company, said this about the company: "We serve women, make wonderful clothes, and now we want to make them sustainable and we want to make nothing but love the result of the work that we do." She lists the following seven commitments that she refers to as the company purpose:[10]

1   Support the well-being of people and the planet through innovation and great design.
2   Use business as a force for change by making clothes that empower women and are responsibly designed from field to factory to closet.
3   To embrace who we are, to innovate, to empower and to be a force of change.
4   To empower us and everyone we connect with to be their best selves as a collective force for positive change.
5   At Eileen Fisher we are creating a world where people have the possibility to be themselves through our products and practices. At our heart is timeless design with timely positive impact.
6   Make good: Connections, choices, impact, design, decisions, clothes, investments, messages.
7   Transform and lead meaningful business, creating products we love, in service of women and the planet.

The company's behavior aligns with these commitments. They pledged that all their cotton and linen would be organic by 2020. They spearheaded an initiative to reduce toxins in dyes used in clothing.[11] And the company has launched their Repair and Care program, focused not only on advising consumers about how to make their clothes last longer, but also on how to recycle rather than discard old clothing.[12] The Eileen Fisher Renew project enables consumers to drop off old clothing at one of their own recycling centers where they reuse the clothing and fabrics for resale, redesign, or to regenerate fabrics.[13] Their website describes their vision using the following words: "For an industry where human rights and sustainability are not the effect of a particular initiative but the cause of a business well run. Where social and environmental injustices are not unfortunate outcomes but reasons to do things differently."[14]

Case: Skanska – values inform choices

No company can do everything. A clear identity embedded into the culture informs decisions about what to pursue and forgo. For example, Skanska, a multinational construction and development company based in Sweden, lives by its purpose and a strong code of ethics. On their website they state the following: "The Skanska Purpose – to build for a better society. Our Skanska values are expected behaviors, anchored in our beliefs and priorities, guiding us in our actions. They serve as a moral foundation and compass." They list their values as: Care for Life, Act Ethically & Transparently, Be Better – Together, and Commit to Customers.[15]

A few years ago, I had the pleasure of facilitating a panel that included Elizabeth Heider, the Chief Sustainability Officer for Skanska U.S.A. She explained how Skanska employs its values to drive their contribution to a more sustainable world. For example, she said that the company will only enter markets where they can live their values. She cited some instances of markets that they exited because of sharp disconnects between what Skanska stands for and what doing business in those markets would require.[16]

Why identity is important

Culture rests on company identity. As you can see from the examples in the previous section, identity guides our commitments, the choices we make, and the systems we put in place. Identity influences how we treat each other inside our organizations as well as how we relate to the world outside of our organizations' boundaries.

Identity as the framework for culture

Leinwand and Mainardi claim that a strong, coherent identity provides the company with a framework for functioning. "It is what drives your entire organization to perform, what makes hiring top talent easier, and what gives you the framework by which to operate the company."[17]

Our research shows that when a clear purpose is central to company identity, the entire internal culture is more positive. In their article, *Clarifying the Meaning of Sustainable Business*,[18] my colleagues, Katrin Muff and Thomas Dyllick, differentiated between companies that set sustainability-related goals aimed at reducing their negative environmental impact and companies that have shifted their focus from doing less harm to doing more good. The latter tend to take on societal challenges. When we compared how employees within these two types of companies view their cultures, we found that those employed in companies focused on doing more good are significantly more positive on items related to trust, encouraging and rewarding innovation, challenging the status quo, and believing that the company values them.[19] Moreover, in a related study, we found that when companies have integrated sustainability into the core of their business models, their employees are significantly more engaged with the company and with their jobs overall.[20]

Identity and relationships with externals

Identity also determines how companies connect with people and institutions outside of their own boundaries. Sustainable companies, to a greater extent than others, tend to connect with a wide variety of stakeholders and care more than others about their reputation. A likely explanation for these differences is that sustainable companies believe they have a role to play in society. Likewise, they view their commitment to sustainability as critical to their long-term success.

How company identity forms and persists

Founders' roles

You may recall that personal identity initially comes from our parents. So too, a company's identity is usually rooted in how its founders conceived it and embedded it into the culture. While identity evolves over time, the original core often endures as it is passed down through myths, stories, and symbols.

Case: Dow – do it better

The story of Dow can serve as a good example of how a company's identity was formed by its founder. Herbert Henry Dow started the Dow Chemical Company in 1897. As both a scientist and an entrepreneur, he built his company around valuing innovation as a key component of the company's identity and cultural foundation. He embedded his life-long passion for solving problems into the culture from the start. Throughout his entire lifetime he continued to research, invent, and innovate, acquiring 107 patents. He always envisioned the company to be "solutions providers." An often-repeated story at Dow is that H.H. Dow liked to say, "If you can't do it better, why do it?"[21]

Herbert Henry Dow's founding philosophy and the ongoing tradition of innovation informs the current company vision that refers to innovation for sustainable solutions for human progress. A few years ago, the company increased its emphasis on citizenship and social responsibility. While citizenship may be a new way of talking about Dow's vision, the desire to find solutions to problems through innovation connects very clearly to the interests and words of H.H. Dow.

Case: IBM – values endure

When he became the leader of Computing Tabulation Recording Company (C-T-R) in 1914, Thomas Watson Sr. created a unique company. He changed the company name to International Business Machines (IBM) in 1924, and the company became known for its values-driven culture. Watson emphasized three basic beliefs:

1   Respect for the individual.
2   Superlative customer service.
3   Pursuit of excellence in all tasks.[22]

While many aspects of the IBM culture have changed to meet the demands of the current times, facets of the original cultural foundation persisted for many years, some would argue right up to the present.

Throughout the 1980s I consulted with IBM. During this time they shifted production from mainframe computers and Selectric typewriters to personal computers (PCs). Their culture, which included a deep commitment to respect for the individual, was very much alive and well. I witnessed examples of this respect and caring in action every day. Throughout these tumultuous times, they continued to operate with their "no layoff" practice. However, they faced the challenge of a skills mismatch between their workforce and the requirements of the transformed organization. My role was to help them develop and implement strategies for enhancing the positive effects of the change while cushioning employees from the negative repercussions.

First, we analyzed who was most likely to be affected by the transition and what the impact might look like. Then we designed a company-sponsored strategy that included career planning, technical and soft skills training, job placements, re-socialization and stress management. These programs embodied the essence of the cultural foundation that Watson Sr. and Jr. had established.

Some have argued convincingly that IBM held on to this culture far too long. When viewed in retrospect, practices such as "no layoffs" very well may have contributed to their business woes. Critics have said that their arrogance prevented them from adapting to new circumstances as the world changed around them. And, as a result, their fortunes fell.

Even though I admire how they handled this transformation from the standpoint of how they treated their employees, I do understand the importance of adapting to change and remaining resilient. The history of IBM reminds us that all companies must adapt and change over time if they are to survive. In 2003, as the company revisited their identity, they modified their values to include:

1   Dedication to every client's success.
2   Innovation that matters – for the company and for the world.
3   Trust and personal responsibility in all relationships.

While the words have changed to reflect the challenges the company faces today, the essence of the new values resembles the old. IBM has changed in many ways over the years. Nonetheless their values-driven identity has remained remarkably stable.

Stories, myths and symbols

Company cultures are passed from one generation to the next through several means, including stories, myths, and symbols.

Cases: stories for sustaining

Myths and stories are powerful ways to sustain identity. I have worked with many organizations where stories are passed down through the years to cement the company's character. Consider how IBM used the word "think" as a slogan and a symbol. They printed it on signs that employees placed on their desks. It was incorporated into their publications and eventually it became an IBM trademark. They even incorporated it into their line of portable personal computers, the ThinkPads. They still refer to their annual business and technology conference as Think.

Likewise, Dow's story of how H.H. Dow said "If you can't do it better, don't do it" is repeated to this day. Similarly, a more recent client maintains the company identity through stories such as how they rallied during the terrorist attacks of 9/11. They claim that they were at their best post 9/11 and after Hurricane Sandy. This organization's identity, and therefore culture, even today, is centered around their ability to work together and get things done in times of crisis.

I'm sure all of us have heard the story (possibly myth) of how two young men, putting a computer together in a garage, founded Apple. These myths and stories become part of the fabric of company identity and can preserve the organizational culture over time. I have learned to listen to the stories and what I can learn about the culture from them.

Identity disconnects

No matter what you tell people about company identity, they will pay attention to what you do. People make inferences about your company by observing actions. And all too often words and deeds are not aligned. For example, Volkswagen claims the following: "For Volkswagen, sustainability means pursuing economic, social and ecological objectives simultaneously and with equal energy. It is our aim to create lasting values, offer good working conditions, and conserve resources and the environment."[23] Yet, after the fact, they admit that they failed to live up to their own standards when they engaged in fraudulent behavior regarding vehicle emissions reporting.

Volkswagen is not the only company with disconnects between what they say and what they do. I have observed many instances of misalignment between words and deeds. Sometimes companies know their descriptions don't match their behaviors. However, other times the descriptions of identity may match behaviors to some extent but not entirely. If the organization itself is disjointed, often described in the business lingo as siloed, actions in different parts of the organization may vary. Thus, the opportunity for disconnects between identity and behavior somewhere in the company abound. In general, the weaker the integration of identity into our business models, operations, and decision-making processes, the greater the chance of behaviors inconsistent with our commitments, especially in larger companies. Let's look at an example.

Case: identity disconnect

A few years ago, I talked with the corporate sustainability officer of a professional services firm about their culture. He was very proud of his company's commitments to social responsibility. He described success stories such as their carbon emissions reduction targets and waste reduction efforts. He was especially proud of their volunteerism program. While I was impressed with their programs, I remember thinking at the time that this work did not seem to be integrated into their core business.

A few years following our conversation, the public learned that the company had lost some of its key employees as well as a few high-profile clients because they advised customers that were climate change deniers. Moreover, they actively helped companies lobby against climate-related regulations. Despite their track record for volunteerism, they appeared to lack a commitment to social responsibility that guided how they conducted business. They suffered bad publicity because of the revelations. Even though they moved quickly to address the problems, their reputation was impaired. They learned that "doing good" in one aspect of the company's work did not cancel out "doing harm" in another. This case serves as a strong example of how social responsibility often consists of a portfolio of initiatives carried out by one person or a department. Under this scenario, it is a bolt-on, meaning that it is peripheral to the company's business model and strategy. When social responsibility is not embedded deep into the way the organization functions, decisions and actions are unlikely to be consistent across the company. And if the public sees these inconsistencies, the company's actions rather than words will hold more sway.

Signaling identity

Company identity cannot be accessed directly. We can neither see it nor touch it. So how do we communicate it to our own employees as well as to the public? Certainly, we announce our identity by what we say and do. But we also signal or announce our identity in many other ways as well.

How we signal identity

Companies signal their identities through logos, advertisements, the look and feel of websites and even workplace design. The authors of *The Value of Corporate Purpose: A Guide for CEOs and Entrepreneurs* argue that purpose can be a source of competitive advantage in that it potentially can drive choices in the marketplace, among other things. However, purpose will provide advantages to companies only if perceived as authentic.[24] Therefore, companies with purpose integrated into their core must have a way to signal it and validate it with the public.

Signaling identity through workplace design

What does your workplace design say about your company's values and priorities? Previously I discussed how Skanska, the sustainable multinational construction and development company, follows its values when determining markets to pursue. In addition, their values have influenced their interest in how buildings affect the people who work in them. According to Chris Pottage, a Skanska Sustainable and Healthy Buildings Officer, the way a building is designed affects the well-being of those who occupy it. On the technical side, design affects the physical environment such as the amount of daylight and fresh air or the level of contaminants in the building.[25] On the experiential side, workplace design affects the degree to which the building provides a view of nature and a wide array of work spaces that promote movement and healthy offices that are welcoming and calming. And, of course, "green" buildings address carbon footprint reduction.[26] Many aspects of a workplace design can signal a sustainable company's identity. The designs communicate what the company cares about to both employees and to the public. Thus, building designs can say a great deal about the authenticity of company commitments.

Recently, I discussed the various ways organizations communicate their identity and brand with Jack Weber, Senior Vice President and Leader of Corporate Workplace Design for Gresham Smith, an architect, engineering, and design practice. Weber contends that a company's brand is about its reputation whereas the culture is about its attitude, beliefs, and behaviors. He says that culture and brand, created by behaviors, should be aligned. Together they comprise the company identity.

Since design can serve as a powerful signal of identity, Weber seeks to understand both culture and brand when designing a workplace. He claims, "It is all about the story. If we know what the story is or what the company wants it to be, we can design the workplace to support it."[27] Therefore he pursues the company "story" as he works with clients. He asks them to define what they would like their employees or their own clients to say about them and their workplace after having worked in it or visited.

After 50 years in business, Gresham Smith has recently gone through its own reflection process to reestablish its purpose and values. Weber said that the new purpose statement is, "Strive to design and plan for community vitality." In his opinion, the purpose and values have not strayed too far from the founders' original vision. The identity has been refined rather than transformed. He claims that the exercise was invaluable for realigning all parts of the company identity and clarifying its brand.

He is aware that a restatement of the identity cannot change actions. However, a strong identity can serve as a powerful guide for behavior. Now that the identity has been refined and aligned, Gresham Smith is in a better position to signal it to their employees and to the public through consistent visual representation and workplace design. And, in Weber's words, "a strong and clear identity guides both culture and branding."

B Corporations: certification of authentic purpose

As I have discussed throughout this chapter, purpose is a significant aspect of a company's identity and can be signaled in several ways. Many socially responsible companies have chosen to become B Corps certified to signal the authenticity of their purpose.

While many avenues exist for establishing the legitimacy of their purpose, a prevalent method is to obtain B Corporation certification by the third party B Labs. Companies pursuing this certification are evaluated for how they have integrated their social purpose with their mission. They must be able to demonstrate their impact on governance, workers, community, and the environment to be certified.[28] While the process can be daunting, the number of applications for certification has been growing since the beginning in 2007.[29] Certification provides a powerful way to signal an authentic purpose. And the process itself creates the motivation and structure to measure whether companies are truly making an impact, and, if not, how they can adjust.

Case: Danone – largest certified B Corps in the world

Some B Corps were organized from the beginning as socially responsible businesses with a clear purpose beyond profits. For example, Danone North America, a business unit of Paris-based multinational food corporation Danone, has always had a clear social purpose. Recently Danone North America, maker of products such as Dannon and Wallaby yogurts, became the largest certified B Corp in the world. They have passed the stringent certification test showing that their business is a force for good.

As with so many other companies, their current culture is built on the foundation established by the founders. Founder and first CEO of parent company Danone, Antoine Ribaud, said,

> Corporate responsibility does not end at the factory gate or the office door. The jobs a business creates are central to the lives of employees, and the energy and raw materials we consume change the shape of our planet.[30]

And he created a company that functioned accordingly. A company does not have to be officially designated as a certified B Corp to be socially responsible. Nevertheless, this certification process is one way to signal an authentic purpose.

Summary and conclusions

Company identity is how those on the inside view themselves and how they present the company to others. When identities are strong, they become the foundational framework for a durable culture. Companies with a social purpose, often referred to as purpose-driven, are likely to have strong identities that resonate in the work environment. Identity usually develops through the values that company founders established from the start. It is passed down over time through stories and symbols. In fact, stories are critical to maintaining as well as changing identity. One way to change the identity is to change the story. However, what companies say about themselves is not as powerful as what they do and how they signal an authentic purpose. When words and actions are inconsistent, a company's reputation is at stake and the identity is meaningless as a clear framework for culture. Without consistency between words and deeds, trust is impossible. And without trust, a company is in trouble. In the next chapter we turn to trust – another foundational building block of culture.

Your turn: assess your company's identity

We are not all CEOs or Chairs of the Board. Yet each of us has some influence over a part of our organizations, whether it is a region, a department, a team, or our own job. I believe that our companies' cultural building blocks influence all else within the organization. Thus, the importance of understanding the history of our companies cannot be overstated, no matter what our role or our area of influence.

Part 1: assess your company's foundational identity

Start to uncover your own company's foundational identity, if it is available to you. Do some research on your company's history and use the chart below to jot down what you find.

Review the history of the company

Complete the following sentences:

The founders described the purpose of the company as:
The founders' dreams for the future (vision) included:

Identify a few of the company's pivotal experiences since the founding

Pick out three or four critical events that you found through your research or that you know about through some other means. Locate these events on the chart/time-line below, starting from the founding of the company and leading up to the current date.

Current identity

Reflect on the questions in the left column in the table below. Use the right column of the table to respond. Your answers should begin to reveal your company's identity.

How do you think people in the organization would describe its purpose?	
What do you claim as your company's values, i.e., what you stand for? (describe the source of this information, e.g., speeches, company website, other).	
Describe one story that people in the company tell each other repeatedly.	
Who does your company claim as your heroes?	
What do your stories and your heroes tell you about the company? For example, we admire heroic individual efforts, we value relationships, we take pride in our ethics.	
What kind of attitudes and behaviors do you reward and punish (either formally or informally)?	

(continued)

(continued)

How do the values that you claim (on your website, in speeches, in advertising) match the values that show up in your stories?	
Where are the disconnects, if any, between what your company says and what it does?	

Part 2: assess your area of influence

Unless you are the CEO or in a formal senior leadership position, identify a part of the organization where you have influence. It may be a region, a department, a team, or your own individual job. Answer the questions in the table below as they relate to your area of influence.

Your area of influence is (region, department, team, job):	
How do you think that the company history has influenced the culture in your part of the organization?	
As you think about your own area of influence, what do you think this area stands for? What are your values?	

What stories about this area do you tell yourselves repeatedly?	
Who are your heroes? How are they similar to or different from your company's heroes overall?	
What do your stories and your heroes tell you about your own part of the organization?	
What kinds of attitudes and behaviors do you reward and punish?	
How do the values that you claim show up in your behaviors?	
Where are the disconnects, if any, between what you claim and what you do?	

As you reflect on your answers in the previous two tables, identify any issues or vulnerabilities that you noticed as you described your company and your area of influence. Jot down your thoughts in the chart below.

Gaps/issues in company:	
Gaps/issues in your area of influence:	

Tool: how to craft a purpose statement

This tool is for those of you who would like to define or redefine the purpose of your area of influence. First, review the qualities of an aspirational purpose statement. Then draft a purpose statement. This may be for the entire company, a region, a department, a team, or your own job. Remember that purpose refers to why the organization, or your part of it, exists in the first place. It is not a description of your business, your goals, or your strategies.

Qualities of an aspirational purpose statement

An aspirational purpose:

Inspires

Employees engage when a clear purpose guides everything else. Engagement soars when people understand how their own work connects with the purpose. Disney leaders have claimed that every employee, no matter what they do, can connect their own work with the company purpose which is to make people happy. No matter whether they work on the grounds, in the cafeterias or in the corporate offices, all can contribute to fulfilling this inspiring purpose.[31]

Remains valid in changing times

A sound purpose transcends the company's latest products and services. Disney started out as a cartoon studio in 1923. The purpose of the company was: "To create happiness for others." Over time, they branched out into resorts and theme parks, television studios, and retail stores, among other ventures. They even purchased a hockey team at one point. Note that today they are still true to their purpose of making people happy even though their mission and business models have changed over the years.

Expands thinking

Suppose Disney's original purpose was to produce cartoons. How might this have limited what they have achieved? However, their purpose of making people happy clearly enabled them to move beyond making cartoons.

Clarifies choices

Recall how Skanska uses its values as a guide for making business choices. Values should guide decisions about what to do and what to forgo.

Your turn: define your purpose

Focus on the parts of the organization that you can influence. Many times, an individual can influence more than one part of the organization. Challenge yourself to identify all the areas that you can influence. You may choose to draft a purpose statement for the entire company, your team, your own work, or several of these areas. Before you begin to write, review how you assessed current purpose and values. Did you have trouble defining the purpose? Is your purpose too narrow, too broad? Does it embody the characteristics of an aspirational purpose or do you need to think bigger? If so, draft a new, more aspirational, purpose statement. Repeat this exercise for each part of the organization where you have influence. End by writing a purpose statement for your own role or job using the following template.

My focus is on the following part of my organization:

_____

Our (my) purpose is:

My role/job is:

The purpose of my role/job is:

Notes

1 Abraham Lincoln quotes. *BrainyQuote.com*, BrainyMedia Inc., 2018, accessed November 1, 2018. Available at: www.brainyquote.com/quotes/abraham_lincoln_121094.
2 Paul Leinwand and Cesare Mainardi, "The Three Elements of a Strong Corporate Identity," *Harvard Business Review*, December 9, 2014. Available at: https://hbr. org/2014/12/the-3-elements-of-a-strong-corporate-identity.
3 Rosabeth Moss Kanter, "How Purpose-Based Companies Master Change for Sustainability," in *Leading Sustainable Change*, eds Rebecca Henderson, Ranjay Gulati, and Michael Tushman (Oxford, UK: Oxford University Press, 2015), 11–139.
4 George Kell and Thomas Reeves, "From Corporate Citizenship to Corporate Statesmanship," *Thomas Reuters*, October 3, 2016. Arabesque website accessed September 8, 2018. Available at: https://arabesque.com/2016/10/03/from-corporate-citizenship-to-corporate-statesmanship.
5 "Business Concept: Vision and Business Idea," Ikea website accessed August 29, 2018. Available at: www.ikea.com/ms/en_SG/this-is-ikea/about-the-ikea-group/index.html.
6 Seventh Generation website, accessed August 29, 2018. Available at: www.seventh-generation.com.
7 Kellogg Company website, accessed September 13, 2018. Available at: www.kellogg company.com/en_US/our-vision-purpose.html.
8 IKEA vision, culture and values, website accessed September 25, 2018. Available at: https://ikea.jobs.cz/en/vision-culture-and-values.
9 "Working at Ikea Overview," Glassdoor website accessed on September 26, 2018. Available at: www.glassdoor.com/Overview/Working-at-IKEA-EI_IE3957.11,15.htm.
10 Conscious Company Media, website accessed on August 15, 2018. Available at: https://consciouscompanymedia.com/sustainable-business/designer-eileen-fisher-on-how-finding-purpose-changed-her-company.

11 Eileen Fisher, "Vision 2020," Eileen Fisher website, accessed September 27, 2018. Available at: www.eileenfisher.com/vision-2020.

12 Keri Ulloa, "Why You Should Recycle Everything in Your Closet," on the Eileen Fisher website, accessed September 27, 2018. Available at: www.eileenfisher.com/repair-and-care/why-you-should-recycle-everything-in-your-closet.

13 Eileen Fisher Renew, website accessed September 27, 2018. Available at: www.eileenfisherrenew.com/our-story.

14 Eileen Fisher website, accessed October 14, 2018. Available at: www.eileenfisher.com/vision-2020.

15 Skanska website, accessed August 29, 2018. Available at: www.usa.skanska.com/who-we-are/about-skanska/our-purpose-and-values.

16 Elizabeth Heider, personal communication with the author (panel), March 11, 2016.

17 Paul Leinwand and Cesare Mainardi, "The Three Elements of a Strong Corporate Identity," *Harvard Business Review*, December 9, 2014. Available at: https://hbr.org/2014/12/the-3-elements-of-a-strong-corporate-identity.

18 Thomas Dyllick and Katrin Muff, "Clarifying the Meaning of Sustainable Business: Introducing a Typology from Business as Usual to True Sustainability," *Organization and Environment* 29, no. 2, (2016): 156–174.

19 Katrin Muff, Kathleen Miller Perkins, Meredith Lepley, and Agnieszka Kapalka, "Culture Differences Between Business as Usual and Sustainable Companies," (Working Paper, 2018).

20 Kathleen Miller Perkins and Meredith Lepley, "Organizational Culture and Sustainability," (Working Paper, 2018).

21 Kathleen Perkins, Robert Eccles, and Mark Weik, "Sustainability at Dow Chemical," *Journal of Applied Corporate Finance: A Morgan Stanley Publication* 24, no. 2, (Spring, 2012): 38–44.

22 Kevin Maney, *The Maverick and his Machine: Thomas Watson, Sr. and the Making of IBM*, (New Jersey: John Wiley and Sons, 2003).

23 Volkswagen website, accessed September 17, 2018. Available at: www.volkswagenag.com/en/sustainability.html.

24 George Serafeim, Sakis Kotsantonis, Daniela Saltzman, and Bronagh Ward, *The Value of Corporate Purpose: A Guide for CEOs and Entrepreneurs*, (kks Advisors and the Generation Foundation, 2017), 9.

25 "How a Healthy Workplace Can Benefit You." Article on Skanska website posted on May 8, 2017 and accessed on October 30, 2018. Available at: https://group.skanska.com/media/articles/how-a-healthy-workplace-can-benefit-you.

26 "Building the Business Case: Health, Well-Being and Productivity in Green Offices," posted by the World Green Building Council on October 26, 2016. Available at: www.worldgbc.org/news-media/building-business-case-health-wellbeing-and-productivity-green-offices.

27 Jack Weber, personal communication with the author, September 27, 2018.

28 Certified B Corporation Certification, website accessed September 27, 2018. Available at: https://bcorporation.net/certification.

29 Serafeim, Kotsantonis, Saltzman, and Bronagh, 2017, 13.

30 "The 1972 Speech: A Milestone of Danone's History Turns Forty," Down to Earth website, accessed September 14, 2018. Available at: http://downtoearth.danone.com/2012/11/16/the-1972-speech-a-milestone-of-danones-history-turns-40.

31 Bruce Jones, "Mission vs. Purpose: What is the Difference?" Disney Institute Blog, April 23, 2015. Available at: www.disneyinstitute.com/blog/mission-versus-purpose-whats-the-difference.

4   Trust and trustworthiness

Chapter purpose

A few years ago, I was working with a company experiencing some struggles internally. As I attempted to schedule time to talk with a cross-section of the organization, I discovered that they feared the interview rooms were bugged. We had to meet in the parking lot! As you might imagine, trust had broken down completely and the organization was barely operational. And, as in most cases, no one event had led to this predicament. The problems were caused by neglect. People across the company had ignored the relationship-building critical to the foundation upon which a company rests. Trust is fragile and cannot be left to chance. And, once lost, trust is hard to rebuild. Over the years I have worked with many broken organizational cultures and I have found that lack of trust was almost always at the root of more than a few of their problems. The purpose of this chapter is to examine how trust or lack of it affects both the internal organizational culture as well as external relationships. The chapter also provides examples of how to build or rebuild trust.

Trust in internal organizational culture

Sustainable cultures demonstrate higher levels of trust and trustworthiness than others. Like identity, trust is a foundational building block of both the internal organizational culture and the company's relationships and reputation with the public. When people inside the organization mistrust each other nothing much gets done and the company is likely to lose the competition for talent. Likewise, the future is bleak for those companies that are viewed as untrustworthy by the public. Customers won't buy their products and services, and communities will not welcome their presence.

Anyone who has ever experienced lack of trust in the workplace knows of the personal and organizational costs. Mistrust creates anxiety, acrimony, and general distress. It takes a toll on people personally and dampens productivity. Those who have other job options are likely to leave, creating a revolving door that further erodes effectiveness. Without trust, people spend time and energy to protect their turf, guard information, and fend off perceived threats.

Why trust is important to internal culture

Trust affects personal well-being and engagement

A trusting environment is good for the employees, which, in turn, is good for the company performance. When people trust each other and their organization they experience a greater sense of well-being and engagement, which leads to greater productivity and higher levels of customer loyalty, among other things. Therefore, it is not surprising that companies with cultures built on trust are more successful.

I don't know about you, but I find it hard to enjoy what I am doing and to fully engage if I don't trust my colleagues. We all know that when people trust each other they feel better about their work and their workplace. And, as in most cases, the research backs up what we have learned from our own practical experiences. Predictably, the studies show a connection between trust, job satisfaction, employee well-being, and engagement. Employee motivation specialist Susanne Jacobs isolated eight organizational factors that, when combined with some environmental considerations, have a significant impact on employee well-being. The factors include:

1   A feeling of belonging and connection.
2   Feeling that they are contributing and are valued.
3   Belief that contributions are recognized and appreciated.
4   Fair and consistent treatment of employees.
5   Belief that they are continuously learning.
6   Belief that they have some control over their own choices.
7   Security in their positions.
8   A clear sense of purpose.[1]

Our research shows that sustainable companies are significantly more likely than others to demonstrate the majority of these eight characteristics. The clearest relationship is between sense of purpose, high levels of trust, and sense of well-being. People who believe that their work is meaningful and that they can trust each other experience the highest levels of well-being. I discuss these connections in greater detail in the next chapter.

Trust is the foundation for collaboration and innovation

Companies today don't stay on top very long without innovating. And successful innovation usually comes from strong collaboration across boundaries, which, of course, requires trust. Our common sense tells us that trust is a must for working with others effectively. And the research backs up this hunch. According to a study conducted by Interaction Associates, Trust Leaders organizations, when compared with Trust Laggards organizations, demonstrated stronger leadership and collaboration. While 65 percent of those in Trust Leaders organizations consider their companies to be innovative, only 14 percent in the Trust Laggards organizations said the same.[2] Likewise, a study by Great Place to Work shows that innovation grows faster when the organizational culture encourages cross-functional and cross-organizational collaboration.[3]

As disruptions in the marketplace have become commonplace, the significance of the trust necessary for collaboration and innovation is indisputable. Trust is especially significant for sustainable companies since they are tackling social and environmental dilemmas, often without known solutions. When people trust each other and the organization, they are more willing to accept the uncertainty and ambiguity. Trust lends some stability to an otherwise uncertain environment.

Types of trust within organizations

The importance of trust cannot be denied. Within an organization, the trust that people have in each other and in the organization itself affects how the company functions. Therefore, building trust internally is a highly consequential responsibility of leadership. To address trust, leaders must understand it. Even though many types of trust exist, I will explore two types that I believe are most relevant to companies: Interpersonal and organizational trust.

Interpersonal trust

How would you describe the people you trust at work? Chances are you would say that they are:

- Ethical and honest.
- Capable of doing their jobs.
- Reliable and follow through on commitments.
- Caring about the well-being of others.

These are typical dimensions of interpersonal trust in the workplace. Interpersonal trust refers to whether people have confidence in each other and believe in the reliability and truthfulness of others. When people trust each other, many aspects of work become easier. For example, conflicts are more easily resolved when interpersonal trust is high.

As my company works with client organizations, we see the real impact of interpersonal trust or lack of it on productivity. Consider the following example.

Case: Urban Company with low interpersonal trust

A while back we worked with a large organization which I will refer to as the Urban Company. This establishment suffered from a culture with a serious lack of interpersonal trust across departmental lines. The leaders of the engineering department hid information from the finance and legal departments because they were fearful that they would create barriers preventing them from getting their work done efficiently and effectively. Likewise, people in the finance and legal departments feared that the engineers would circumvent their processes.

This lack of trust created an atmosphere where employees were afraid to talk with people outside of their departments. The engineers went to great lengths to hide what they were doing while the finance and legal departments spent much time and effort in trying to find out what was going on in engineering. Groups were constantly seeking ways to undermine the others. We heard stories of senior team members refusing to meet with others they didn't like or trust. The list of grievances was long and serious. The dysfunction led to wasted time, mistakes, and inefficiencies. As a result, the entire organization was affected by the general upheaval.

The Urban Company had a social mission focused squarely on the benefit of the community where they were located. However, a workforce cannot optimize positive impact on their customers and communities while people within the organization, especially the leaders, actively undermine each other. Interpersonal trust is fundamental to excellent performance and maximum positive results in all organizations. It is even more vital in organizations that seek to be sustainable and socially responsible because balancing profits and purpose is not easy. Success requires widespread buy-in across the organization. And true engagement with the vision is unlikely when trust is lacking. The best path forward for sustainable companies is to build trust intentionally across the organization.

Organizational trust

While interpersonal trust refers to the faith that people have in each other, organizational trust is about the confidence that people hold in the company overall.

- **Belief in the competency and ethics of leaders**

  Our research shows that employees judge the trustworthiness of their organizations through more than one lens. The first factor involves the level of confidence that employees feel concerning leaders' knowledge and ethics. When employees believe that their leaders have a profound knowledge of the company's business and industry, as well as strong personal values and commitments to a purpose, they trust the leaders to make good decisions that will keep the company strong and competitive.

- **Perceptions of fair treatment**

  Another factor critical to organizational trust is whether people perceive the treatment of employees to be consistent and fair rather than capricious and unjust. Of course, employees will view their organizations as trustworthy only if they think that systems affecting them are fair. Therefore, if they see favoritism toward certain groups of people, or policies that they believe have a negative impact on their quality of life, they are unlikely to trust the organization.

Case: Entrepreneurial Company with low organizational trust

Recently a client, which I will refer to as the Entrepreneurial Company, found out the hard way what happens when company practices are perceived to be unfair. This small organization was growing very fast and clearly outperforming their competitors. But they began hiring many new people rapidly and they were not taking the time to train them adequately. They believed people should be self-reliant and learn on their own, just as their current employees had done when the company was a small start-up. New employees were thrown into situations for which they were not ready, and the more seasoned workers were unable to help them much because of growing time pressures.

This company also tended to select people for supervisory positions based on a "buddy system." People were promoted into supervisory and managerial roles with very little if any preparation. As a result, they were ill equipped to manage. Employees reported that their new supervisors were disrespectful and incompetent. The trust that the company had experienced previously had eroded to the degree that they faced an insurrection in the workforce.

People had lost confidence in the organization and its leaders. They questioned the fairness of hiring and promotional practices and doubted the capabilities of those who were put into positions of authority. These destructive outcomes occurred because the company had fallen into the common trap of believing that the methods that had worked for them when they were small would continue to work as they grew. Their growth required new approaches and a different culture. Because they were not quick to recognize the need to change, this highly successful company risked becoming the victim of low organizational trust.

Levels of trust within organizations today

I'm sure we can all agree that both interpersonal and organizational trust are more desirable than mistrust. Most likely many of us have experienced how trust or lack of it affects our own welfare and has a negative impact on what we can accomplish as a company. Nevertheless, far too few companies consciously foster trust. Even though many leaders advocate the importance of trust, our research shows that when employees assess the characteristics of their companies' cultures, trust comes out near the bottom of their ratings.

Levels of trust are low in general

In 2016 we analyzed our entire database developed through the administration of our culture assessment instrument over the years. We looked at which of the many factors in organizational cultures received the highest and the lowest ratings to better assess patterns in strengths and weaknesses across companies. Trust was among the lowest of all culture ratings throughout our entire data base. Likewise, ratings of the effectiveness of people working across departments was also among the lowest recorded. Taken together, these two results, while disturbing, make sense. Of course, when trust is low, collaborating across boundaries will also be difficult. Given the centrality of trust to so many other aspects of culture and performance, these dismal results should cause concern.

Levels of trust are higher in sustainable organizations

Even though trust tends to be too low in companies in general, it is significantly higher in sustainable companies overall. This difference is not surprising. For a company to successfully carry out its commitments to a purpose beyond profits, employees must trust each other, the organization itself, and its leaders. Without trust, employees are unlikely to commit to a vision, let alone engage with it. When a company pursues a purpose, they need everyone to be on board.

In one of our earliest studies we compared the cultures of companies with a strong reputation for sustainability (sustainable companies) with those with weaker reputations (traditional). We found that in the sustainable companies 47 percent strongly agreed that organizational trust was high, whereas only 6 percent strongly agreed in the traditional organizations. Likewise, in our most recent study we compared the cultures of companies at three different levels of commitment to sustainability. We found that companies with the highest level of commitment to sustainability, those that were purpose-driven, demonstrated higher levels of organizational trust than the companies at the lower levels of commitment.[4]

Our studies show that socially responsible and sustainable companies foster trust by valuing employees, honoring commitments, and aligning decisions and actions with professed values. These companies have a clear strategy for establishing and maintaining trust because they are aware that, without it, the organization is unlikely to succeed. Within a culture of trust, employees feel that their contribution is appreciated, and, therefore, they are more likely to work actively to achieve the company goals.[5]

Case: Japanese American Company: a strategy for building trust

Our client, which I will refer to as the Japanese American Company, is in the transportation industry with corporate headquarters on the East Coast of the United States. This company has an interesting history and some unique cultural challenges. The East Coast team came together in the 1980s to bid on a public-sector transportation project. At this point, they did not view themselves as a long-term, cohesive company. They won the bid but still viewed their work as a project only. They set up separate facilities for their engineers, administrative, and production staff. In addition to their headquarters, they had another manufacturing facility in the Midwest. After succeeding in achieving the goals of this first project, they decided to form a more cohesive, longer-term company to bid on similar ventures. They wanted to run the business as one company and not a collection of different offices and individual people scattered across several buildings in two states.

This company was quite diverse from the beginning. This Japanese/American company had a senior management team with members from both countries, thus challenging them to understand and blend the two cultures. In addition, their employees represented many ethnic groups and spoke several languages. On top of this diversity within their East Coast offices, their partner facility in the Midwest added another level of cultural differences to the mix. Thus, the loose organization was composed of many subcultures divided by functions, regions, national cultures, and ethnic differences.

When my company first became involved with the Japanese American Company, the senior leadership team's goal was to bring together the various parts of the organization and create a cohesive, smoothly functioning, viable operation. They drafted a vision for their organization and listed some ways in which they hoped to achieve it. For example, they wanted to implement new management information and control systems, become process rather than functionally focused, formalize and strengthen their communications, and clarify roles for each level of management. They wanted to professionalize management and operate more like an American company. And they wanted to increase employee involvement and commitment. They realized that their ability to achieve their goals rested on the level of trust that they could build throughout their very complex organization. They decided to start by working on the trust within their own leadership team.

Senior leaders from both the Midwest and the East Coast met together in a retreat setting to develop a team mission statement reflecting their collective responsibilities for enabling a trusting culture. Their team mission stated:

> The Japanese American Company Leadership Team will provide unified leadership, and stability to company employees through planning, setting clear common goals, communicating effectively to achieve profit goals, quality products, excellent service, and credibility to customers. We will accomplish this mission by being honest, listening, and maintaining integrity, trusting and supporting each other. We will communicate consistently with one unified voice.

They realized that trust had to start with their own team. They determined that they would need more face-to-face meetings and better ways to get to know each other and communicate. They committed to replacing "management by exception" with some clear guidelines and policies for promotions, decision-making, and dealing with conflict. They began to draft strategies for building trust among and between the many subcultures in their organization. And they pledged to speak with one voice as a leadership team.

Upon addressing their own trust-related issues, the leadership team established strategies for engaging other levels of management and employees in trust-building. Their strategies included more interaction across functions and some specific methods for helping all groups understand where they fit in the big picture. They wanted all to understand how every group contributed to the company outcomes. As a result of their efforts, people became more appreciative of how each group depended on the others and furthered the company purpose. Through these work-related activities and some celebratory social events, this company created a sense of community.

As their organization culture changed, this company gained more credibility from their project performance, high technology, and vehicle reliability. They committed to bringing more environmentally friendly modes of transportation to their markets in the United States and around the world. And, in 2017, they secured their biggest contract ever – an order worth approximately $1.45 billion. This company illustrates the power of building trust intentionally across an organization.

Whose job is it to build trust?

Everyone in a company is responsible for building a trusting environment. However, leaders in formal positions of authority have a specific mandate to establish trust.

The Edelman company, a communications firm, has been administering a global trust survey for many years. And the 2018 survey provided both good and bad news. First the bad news. Within the general population of the U.S., trust overall in institutions has dropped more than ever before in the history of Edelman's research. The good news is that 72 percent trust their employers to do what is right.[6] People who participated in the trust survey also asserted that top-level leaders are responsible for deepening trust in their organizations. In fact, close to 70 percent said that building trust is the CEO's number one job.[7] Do we, in formal positions of leadership, deserve our employees' trust? And are we willing to embrace the responsibility of building it throughout our organizations? These are questions for all of us to ponder.

How to build trust internally

The lower levels of trust that show up in our research may mean that we, as leaders, aren't very good at building it. As the Japanese American Company case illustrated, trust doesn't always develop naturally. Sometimes it requires intentional effort. Trust is fragile. It must be nurtured. Once lost, it is hard to rebuild.

Intentional trust-building

Building trust, both interpersonal and organizational, is not effortless. Even with clear intentions, trust-building can be a slow process. Yet both organizational and interpersonal trust are necessary for any company to meet the challenges of our world's constantly changing landscape. The most trusting cultures intentionally work to build it. Trust rarely grows by default. It takes hard work, new mindsets, and a willingness to take some risks.

To stay relevant, our companies must be able to attract talent and build the kind of collaboration that leads to innovation. Therefore, trust is even more critical in sustainable companies that often rely on innovation to carry out their missions. In an article that I wrote with my colleagues some years ago, we stated,

> Trust grows when people perceive that they are part of a collective effort to deliver value to stakeholders in a way that contributes to the betterment of their world. Work becomes more meaningful and people become more engaged and productive.[8]

Commit to transparency

Transparency cultivates trust. This means that organizations must share information concerning intentions, strengths, weaknesses, successes, and shortcomings with employees and with the public. Yes, this makes the organization and the individuals in it somewhat vulnerable. Yet, without transparency, trust is unlikely to grow. How often do you trust people who only share information that allows them to hold on to power or makes them look good? The relationship between transparency and trust works in both directions. Transparency builds trust and trust is a prerequisite for ongoing transparency. When we hoard information, trust spirals down. As we share with others, trust builds. It takes trust to feel comfortable with transparency and it takes transparency to build trust.

Take risks

Trust requires some risk-taking because we must start somewhere. Even with the risk, leaders must adopt the attitude that their colleagues are trustworthy and act accordingly unless proved wrong. As Ernest Hemingway once said, "The best way to find out if you can trust somebody is to trust them."[9]

Nourish trust through collaboration

Once established, trust must be sustained purposefully. Trust develops through interactions and experiences. Productive collaboration both internally and across organizational boundaries provides both. In our own consulting work, we have found that collaboration is a cornerstone of successful trust-building strategies.

Distribute power

When power is distributed rather than held by only those who are in positions of formal authority, people are more willing to engage and participate to achieve common goals. Indeed, trust requires widespread involvement in setting the collective rules of engagement.

Invest in employees

As power is distributed throughout an organization, everyone needs the knowledge and skills to handle it well. An investment in the training and development of employees can equip them for the added responsibilities of participating in decision-making.

Challenge the status quo

In trusting companies, people are expected to share their points of view and engage in healthy debates as a natural part of decision-making. Challenging the status quo is a way of life. Some companies establish protocols for ensuring that these debates take place.

Identify causes of problems collectively

Everyone in the company should have the opportunity to participate in examining what is working and what is not. All should accept some responsibility for their part of any problems uncovered, no matter what their levels or roles in the organization.

Design the future collectively

To build trust, companies may facilitate widespread participation in figuring out how to pursue a vision or solve a problem. In circumstances where trust has been broken, the best approach to fixing it is to work together to assess what might be done differently to prevent these situations in the future. Issues to explore could include whether some of the systems might need to be overhauled or behaviors might need to change.

Communicate, communicate, communicate

Companies must communicate commitments, discuss problems, and explore opportunities – not just once but repeatedly in many different forums. Even when you think that you have communicated enough, communicate more. No amount of communication is too much when building trust.

Hold each other accountable

All of us must be accountable for our own behavior. We must show respect, uphold our commitments, keep confidences, and consider the well-being of others as well as our own. And all of us must align our behavior to the collective values we share in the company.

Trustworthiness and reputation with externals

Companies' relationships with people and institutions outside of their own boundaries depend on the degree to which they are regarded as trustworthy. The organization Trust Across America is so convinced of the importance of trustworthiness that they have developed a methodology for ranking and rating publicly traded companies on five quantitative measures of trustworthy business behaviors including: Financial stability and strength, accounting conservativeness, corporate integrity, transparency, and sustainability. They have worked with this framework for many years and have found that while low-trust companies can do well for the short term, they do not perform as well over the longer term. In the long run, high-trust companies tend to show faster decision-making, higher levels of innovation, greater employee retention, and cost savings from improving operational efficiencies.[10]

These measures translate into more positive business outcomes. Trustworthy companies perform better than others. According to Interaction Associates Inc., companies that are Trust Leaders grew revenue two and a half times faster than the Trust Laggards.[11]

Relationship between internal organizational trust and external reputation

The public is likely to judge the trustworthiness of a company by several factors such as the quality of its products and services, whether it stands by its promises, and the degree to which the company has a positive impact on society. However, one of the most powerful determinants of company reputation is how employees talk about their employers to others outside of the organization. While people may not always have faith in the reliability of companies' press releases, they do believe what they hear about companies from their employees. The 2017 Edelman Trust Barometer showed that 64 percent of the respondents believe information about a company that has been leaked from within.[12]

Most people care about their organization's reputation, especially employees of sustainable companies. My research reveals that when employees hold their companies in high esteem they want the public to do so as well. Proud employees can become their company's best ambassadors. The relationship between public and employee perceptions of a company works both ways. When employees view their organization as ethical and trustworthy, the public is likely to share their view. And, conversely, when the company is regarded as trustworthy by the public, its employees are more likely to have confidence in it.[13]

Let's look at a case where employees' lack of trust in their organization damaged the company's reputation with the public.

Case: Southern Company damaged reputation

A few years ago, we worked with an organization where lack of organizational trust was pervasive. I will call this organization the Southern

Company. We were surprised by the problems because this company had a clear purpose and a strong social mission. They were in an industry that had been disrupted by technology, hence their future depended on creating the necessary technological innovations to offset this challenge. Such creative innovation usually occurs through the kind of deep workplace collaboration that is dependent on trust. However, the employees did not trust the organization. They believed that the company was too hierarchical, the management style too directive, and that hiring and promotions were based on personal connections and favoritism.

I found out how these perceptions damaged the company's reputation with the public purely by coincidence. I was advising a young colleague about his career options. We were talking about his aspirations and the companies he most admired when he brought up this very well-known organization, the Southern Company. He did not know that we were working with them. He mentioned that he, and everyone else he knew, would not seek work with them because of their reputation. And I found that my young colleague wasn't the only job seeker who was steering clear of this company. Apparently, the employees had been spreading the word about what they perceived to be an undesirable culture. Young people in the job market had listened to them. After hearing a similar story about the Southern Company several times, I concluded that, over the long run, they would struggle to hire the kind of talent they needed to innovate. Given the disruption in their industry, they were highly dependent on innovation. And innovation depends on talent. Therefore, their reputation with the public might very well endanger their future.

Summary and conclusions

Trust, both interpersonal and organizational, serves as the foundation required for everything else in a company to work. Leaders should never take trust for granted. Building and maintaining trust must be an intentional process. While everyone is responsible for preserving trust, leaders in formal positions of authority are especially accountable for protecting it.

Sustainable companies have higher levels of trust internally than others. This may be because they engage in some specific behaviors and practices to intentionally solidify trust within their organizations. For example, they expect everyone to challenge the status quo and they are committed to transparent and ongoing communications. They tend to be more collaborative and depend on employee participation – practices that build trust.

People in sustainable companies care more than others about their reputation with the public. And a company's reputation depends on trust and trustworthiness. When employees trust their organization, they are more likely to become advocates for it. This advocacy is critical for building a company's reputation with the public since employees' communications about their companies carry much weight with public opinion.

Your turn: assess trust in your workplace

Let's begin by taking a closer look at trust in your company currently. Trust translates into how employees experience their workplaces. Perceptions of trust levels are likely to vary according to the perceivers' position in the company. Therefore, to get a true picture of what people think of the culture, you should solicit input from a cross-section. If you find variations, your task is to determine why these differences exist.

Remember that trust in the workplace can fluctuate from time to time due to many factors including who is in charge, whether the company is stable or in crisis, and many other circumstances. Therefore, plan to take the pulse of the workforce and workplace periodically. You should never take trust for granted. You must assume that rebuilding lost trust will take intentional effort and time.

How others view trust in your workplace

If your organization is mid to large size: Start by reviewing websites that enable prospective employees to research your company based on what your current and previous employees are saying. These sites can provide you with insight into how your company's workplace environment is perceived. Some sites to check out include Glassdoor, Indeed, and Twitter. Glassdoor and Indeed include comments from employees about pros and cons of working for the company. You can search Twitter to see if/what employees and the public might be posting about the company. Of course, the sites aren't perfect. There may be ways to remove negative posts and stuff the ballot box with positives. Nevertheless, I think that doing a search for your company on these sites can provide you with some insights about the environment in your company if you are cautious in your interpretations. Answer the following questions based on what you find.

Question	Comments
Do the pros outweigh the cons or vice versa? (Hint: Look at the overall ratings that Glassdoor and Indeed provide.)	
Do the reviews refer to issues such as how managers treat employees and whether employees feel valued? What can you conclude about trust?	

What, if anything, do the reviews say about the leaders' expertise and knowledge? Do people trust that they are competent?	
Did you find anything that might reflect upon whether your employees view the company as trustworthy? Ethical?	
What are your main takeaways?	

How you view trust in your workplace

Questions	Answers	Your thoughts
Interpersonal trust		
Do you think people in this organization trust each other overall? What leads you to this conclusion? Can you give some examples?		
Do people show respect for each other?		
Overall, do people throughout the company view leaders' and managers' behaviors towards employees as fair?		

(continued)

(continued)

Do people generally do what they say? Are there exceptions? If so, describe.		
Do you think that people in this organization collaborate well with others? Can you explain your answer by giving some examples?		
Do you believe that most people in this organization are ethical and honest?		
Do people in this organization care about the welfare of others for the most part?		
Organizational trust		
Does the company follow through on its commitments to employees?		
Do most employees feel valued by the company and its leaders? How do you know?		

Do most people in the organization care about the company's reputation with the public? Are people in this organization proud of it overall?		
Does the organization encourage the expression of multiple perspectives on issues? Can you give a couple of examples that support your opinion?		
Are the company's policies viewed as fair?		
Does the company meet your expectations by and large?		
Main takeaways:		

Notes

1 Susanne Jacobs, *Employee Motivation: Is Trust the Answer*, Unum, August 27, 2013. Available at: www.unum.co.uk/hr/employee-motivation-is-trust-the-answer.

2 "Building Workplace Trust," Interaction Associates Inc. 2014, 16: 21–22. Available at: http://interactionassociates.com/sites/default/files/research_items/Trust%20 Report_2014_15IA_0.pdf.

3 "Innovation by All: The New Flight Plan for Elevating Ingenuity, Accelerating Performance and Outpacing Rivals," *Great Place to Work*, July 24, 2018. Available at: www.greatplacetowork.com/resources/whitepapers/innovation-by-all.

4 Katrin Muff, Kathleen Miller Perkins, Meredith Lepley, and Agnieszka Kapalka, "Culture Differences Between Business as Usual and Sustainable Companies," Working Paper, 2018.

5 Kathleen Perkins and Meredith Lepley, "Meta Data Analysis of Sustainability Culture and Leadership Assessment (SCALA)," unpublished manuscript, 2016.

6 "Executive Summary," 2018 *Edelman Trust Barometer*, 3. Available at: http://cms. edelman.com/sites/default/files/2018-02/2018_Edelman_TrustBarometer_ Executive_Summary_Jan.pdf.

7 2018, *Edelman Trust Barometer*, 4.

8 Robert Eccles, Kathleen Miller Perkins and George Serafeim, "How to Become a Sustainable Company," *MIT Sloan Management Review* (Summer 2012), 53, no. 4, 43–50.

9 Ernest Hemingway quotes. *BrainyQuote.com*, Xplore Inc., 2018, accessed October 1, 2018. Available at: www.brainyquote.com/quotes/ernest_hemingway_383691.

10 "Trust Across America: A New Framework for Trustworthy Business Behavior," Trust Across America, website accessed September 30, 2018. Available at: www. trustacrossamerica.com/about.shtml.

11 Interaction Associates Inc. 2014, 16. Available at: http://interactionassociates.com/ sites/default/files/research_items/Trust%20Report_2014_15IA_0.pdf.

12 Tamara Snyder and Megan Barstow, "Looking Inward to Rebuild Trust," Edelman website, accessed September 8, 2018. Available at: www.edelman.com/post/looking-inward-to-rebuild-trust.

13 Kai Lamertz and Davashessh P. B. Have, "Employee Perceptions of Organisational Legitimacy as Impersonal Bases of Organisational Trustworthiness and Trust," *Journal of Trust Research*, (April, 2017), 2–7, no. 2, 129–149. Available at: http://doi.org/10.1 080/21515581.2017.1304220.

Part II

The nature of sustainable cultures

The purpose of Part II is to examine in greater detail the components of culture that rest on the foundational building blocks we explored in Part I. These components include internal culture, external relationship, and change capacity. In Chapter 5 we look at what a sustainable internal organizational culture looks like and examine the role of purpose in driving engagement. Chapter 6 turns to how sustainable companies engage with those external to their companies and digs into the nature of their relationships. Chapter 7 begins by observing that sustainable companies have stronger track records for change than others. This chapter examines specific capabilities that could account for their superiority in handling change.

The nature of sustainable cultures

5   Internal organizational culture

From purpose to engagement

Chapter purpose

Steve Jobs once said,

> Your work is going to fill a large part of your life, and the only way to be truly satisfied is to do what you believe is great work. And the only way to do great work is to love what you do.[1]

That is why the internal culture of our organizations is so important. Culture plays a crucial role in whether we are excited about our work or dread doing it.

Employees are more engaged in sustainable cultures. Chapter 1 included the cultural profile of sustainable companies along with the specific qualities that differentiate them from others. This chapter provides evidence that this profile is related to higher levels of employee engagement. The purpose of this chapter is to dig deeper into these distinguishing characteristics and to explore how employee engagement results.

Profile of a sustainable internal culture

The internal cultures of sustainable companies differ from others. These cultures rest on a strong foundation of character-driven leadership, purposeful identity, and trust. When compared with other companies, the specific qualities found in their internal cultures lead to higher levels of employee engagement. Figure 3, Profile of a sustainable internal culture, summarizes these distinctive qualities.

How qualities of sustainable internal cultures relate to engagement

While too many people dislike their jobs and/or their employers, many of us love what we do and where we work. What makes the difference in how we feel about our work? Apparently internal organizational culture has much to do with it. And the internal cultures of sustainable companies tend to be more engaging than others. In sustainable companies, employees trust that the vision

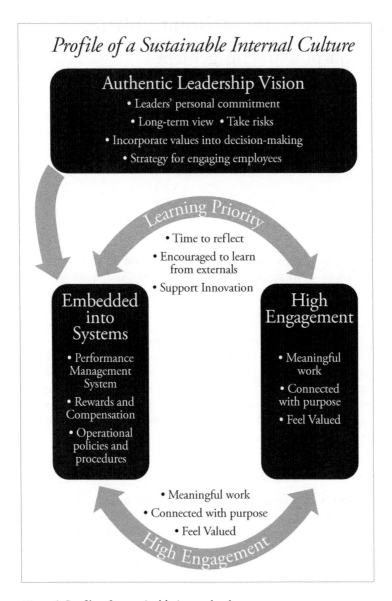

Figure 3 Profile of a sustainable internal culture

is authentic because their leaders' personal commitments show up in their behaviors. For instance, they make long-term commitments, take some risks, and incorporate the company's professed values into their decision-making. Moreover, these companies have specific strategies for engaging employees in the purpose and vision.

Continuous learning is a high priority in sustainable internal cultures. Employees are encouraged to take time to reflect and learn on the job. The company also urges them to learn from people and institutions external to their company boundaries. The emphasis on a culture of continual learning supports their strong commitments to innovation. Most likely these companies foster innovation to find new solutions to the societal problems that they tackle.

Sustainable companies make their identity real by embedding it into the policies, processes, and operations of the company, including the performance management and compensation systems. As a result, employees are more likely to understand how their own work connects with the purpose and vision. Employees in sustainable companies tend to feel valued and believe that their contributions will be rewarded.

Sustainable companies enable employees to use their strengths to carry out work that they view as meaningful. The more meaningful their work, the higher their levels of engagement, that is, their level of emotional attachment to the work and the companies. Because of the company's embedding, connecting, and valuing, employees come to believe that the company's commitment to becoming sustainable is critical to its future.

Case: Procter and Gamble's sustainable culture

The strong relationships between a positive culture, purpose-driven employees, strong brand, and business performance are particularly noteworthy at consumer products giant P&G.

In 2017 P&G was named one of America's best corporate citizens.[2] Their citizenship efforts fall under the following groups:

- Community impact.
- Diversity and inclusion.
- Gender equality.
- Environmental responsibility.

Procter and Gamble has very specific goals for each of the four groups. And according to their *2017 Citizenship Report*, they are making progress in all of them.[3]

The P&G culture is famous for its emphasis on trust, initiative, meaningful work, and agility.[4]

In P&G's *2017 Citizenship Report*, CEO David Taylor stated, "We treat all employees with respect and encourage them to bring their full selves to work."[5] He went on to say that P&G has joined with 300 other companies to form the CEO Action for Diversity and Inclusion initiative. The three areas of focus include:

1 Creating a trusting workplace for dialogue.
2 Understanding unconscious bias.
3 Sharing best practices.

In P&G's first *Citizenship Report* released in 2016, Taylor stated,

> Over my career, I have come to realize the much broader impact a company like P&G can have on the world. Everything we touch, we can help make better. We, along with our partners, can be a positive force for good. This happens when we improve consumers' lives with our brands and products, when we act with integrity and honesty in our business dealings, when we create jobs and economic growth, when we use our voice to encourage meaningful dialogue, when we donate our time and resources to make a positive impact in the communities where we live and work, and when we improve the environmental impact of our products and operations.[6]

In these statements Taylor described his vision for the P&G culture. Taylor is very clear that this is the way P&G will conduct business and deliver results.

Meaningful work and inner work life

Internal organizational culture influences our thoughts and feelings about our work as well as how we perform it. When we are engaged, that is, emotionally attached to our work and our companies, we are less likely to leave, we experience higher levels of job satisfaction, and we perform better. As a result, our companies accomplish more as well. As I mentioned previously, employees' engagement with their work is related to their beliefs that it is meaningful.

Meaningful work comes from making a difference

Meaningful work is important to all of us. In fact, a study conducted by the IBM Workforce Institute found that meaningful work contributes more than anything else to a positive employee experience.[7] While the conditions that define meaningful work may not be the same for everybody, I have found some common themes. People want work to contribute to company success and to making the world a better place. Although Millennials express the strongest needs for these kinds of contributions, this desire shows up in all age groups in the workforce.[8]

A few years ago, I had the opportunity of working with most of the managers in a large technology company. My work was part of a program to teach managers how to coach their employees. We were discussing motivation when I asked them to describe what was most important to them in their jobs – what excites them about their work, and what would keep them from leaving the company. While most people mentioned more than one factor, almost all of them said that they wanted their work to "make a difference." Upon my probing for greater clarity, they told me that they want to know that they are contributing to their company's success and to the betterment of the world. Since we spend close to a third of our lives at work, no wonder we want it to be meaningful.

Meaningful work, motivation, and engagement

Harvard professor Theresa Amabile and her colleague Steve Kramer conducted several studies on inner work life – or how people feel about work. They looked at what motivates employees to feel good about their work. Their research shows that the most significant determinant of feeling engaged on the job is the degree to which employees believe they are making progress on significant work.

Moreover, Amabile and Kramer's research shows that a positive inner work-life experience influences performance. They say that, "Inner work life has a profound impact on workers' creativity, productivity, commitment, and collegiality."[9] People put more effort into their work, including extra time and brainpower, when they are motivated to do it. Amabile and Kramer define motivation as "a combination of a person's choice to do some task, their desire to expend effort doing it, and their drive to persist with that effort."[10] They describe the three most relevant sources of motivation as:

1   Extrinsic – doing something to obtain something else like money, benefits, or rewards.
2   Intrinsic – doing the work for the love of it – because it is interesting, satisfying, or challenging.
3   Relational or altruistic – doing the work because it involves connecting with and providing value to others.

Our inner work experience, both intrinsic and relational/altruistic motivation, affects our levels of engagement.

Employee engagement

Employee engagement within sustainable cultures is striking. And since engagement is closely related to company performance, it is important to a company's long-term success. Therefore, I will take a closer look at engagement, what it means and how it shows up in sustainable companies.

Over the years I have studied employee engagement through both my research and practice. I have also reviewed what others have to say about the topic. Yet, I still have a hard time finding any consensus on its meaning. The concept of engagement is confusing because companies use the term to represent many things and to explain almost everything. Nevertheless, I can draw a few conclusions about engagement with confidence. Engagement is not a program. It cannot be a publicity-seeking initiative or a way to cut costs. Engagement does not come from a company scorecard nor from a profit and loss statement. A healthy paycheck and adequate benefits, while important, will not lead us to engage with our work. Engagement comes from passion about what we are doing, and passion comes from purpose. We are much more likely to be enthusiastic about our work when we know why we are doing it and our "why" includes more than "because we must."

What is employee engagement?

Some definitions focus on internal perceptions while others look at observable behaviors. Several definitions emphasize motivation, while some concentrate on well-being. Engagement has been equated with job satisfaction and ambition. The website HR.com defines it as "our willingness to give our best at work."[11] Wikipedia says that it is "the nature of the relationship between an organization and its employees."[12] No wonder we are not clear about what the term really means.

My working definition of engagement corresponds with the Gallup organization's description. They have studied employee engagement for years and define it as follows: "Engaged employees are those who work with passion and feel a profound connection to their company. They drive innovation and move the organization forward."[13]

Likewise, I characterize engagement as our emotional connection to our work and our workplace. I believe that it is more than satisfaction with our jobs. It is about excitement for our work and the delight that we take in doing it. It is job satisfaction plus enthusiasm and commitment.

What does engagement look like?

Over the years, I have worked with the Miller team to assess employee engagement systematically using structured methodologies. However, even before we do the formal assessment, I usually have a sense of the level of engagement in the organization, and my first impressions often prove to be correct. When employees are engaged, the energy in the workplace is palpable. People are eager to talk about their work. They collaborate across organizational boundaries and share information freely. They are proud of their accomplishments and tenacious in addressing challenges. I witness their problem-solving on white boards in meeting rooms and charts on the factory floor. I see evidence of their camaraderie in break rooms and lunch rooms. Many times, they cheerfully stay at their desks after hours to complete a task that has enthralled them. I have concluded that when we are engaged in our work, we feel more alive.

Why engagement is important

Employee engagement is no longer merely a "nice to have." It is a "must have." Over the past few years research has shown unequivocally the power of employee engagement. Engagement affects individual performance, employees' sense of well-being, and company outcomes.

Engagement and individual performance

Evidence shows that our emotional connection with our work influences our performance. For example, engaged employees are willing to put in more time to complete their work, sometimes referred to as discretionary effort, and less likely to leave their jobs.[14] A thorough review of the research on engagement up through year 2014[15] concluded that while the relationship between engagement and individual behaviors and outcomes is complex, strong evidence across many studies shows that the more engaged employees perform their jobs better than less engaged employees. Engaged employees are more creative and innovative, and they are better organizational citizens – for example, more willing to help others and to keep the organization's best interests in mind. On the other hand, people who are disengaged at work are more likely to act in ways that could harm the organization.

Engagement and well-being

In addition to the relationships between engagement and job performance, higher levels of engagement are associated with stronger levels of well-being. The Gallup organization reports that when employees feel engaged they are more satisfied with their lives in general than those who are not engaged. And, on the other hand, workers who are "actively disengaged" – emotionally disconnected from their work and workplace – are more likely to experience health issues such as physical pain and depression.[16]

Engagement and company outcomes

You don't have to search for reasons to embrace employee engagement in your companies. According to Gallup "engaged employees produce better business outcomes – across industries, company sizes and nationalities, and in good economic times and bad."[17] Engaged employees are important to our companies' success because they are more committed and more productive. Think about how much harder and smarter you work when you are engaged in it rather than just completing tasks to get to the end of the day. In a 2013 study Gallup compared work units with the most engaged employees with work groups whose employees were disengaged. They found that those business units in the top half of the engagement range nearly doubled their odds for success. Their profits were better, as was the value of their stock.[18] Companies with a highly engaged workforce outperformed their peers by 147 percent in earnings per share. Unfortunately, Gallup's studies found that 87 percent of employees world-wide are not engaged in their work.[19]

What can we conclude about engagement? The concept is somewhat muddled. Nevertheless, engagement is important because it is closely connected with superior individual performance, a greater sense of well-being, and better company outcomes.

Commitment to purpose leads to engagement

What prompts engagement? Employees' trust in the company leaders, relationships with their managers, opportunities for growth and development, and recognition and rewards are all related to engagement.[20] In addition, engagement comes from employees' opportunities to use their strengths as well as their understanding of work-related expectations.[21] The list is long. However, two of the strongest and most significant drivers of engagement are:

1   Organizational commitments to a purpose beyond profits.
2   Positive organizational culture to support the purpose.

My own research shows that a purpose-driven vision reinforced through leaders' consistent and aligned behavior is a strong determinant of employee engagement. Employees are most convinced of true company commitment to the vision when its leaders integrate commitments into the decision-making processes and take measured risks in pursuit of the purpose. Likewise, employees look for leaders' willingness to incorporate sustainability into their decision-making before they are convinced of an authentic commitment.

Case: Benevity strives to change the world through employee engagement in "goodness"

Benevity is the global leader in corporate social responsibility and employee engagement software. They claim that their products power corporate "Goodness" programs, which include giving, volunteering, grantmaking, and other prosocial actions. The four million plus people using their solutions come from some of the world's most iconic brands. The company describes its philosophy as follows:

> Goodness (combined with great technology!) has a transformative power that enables businesses to truly engage with their people, unify company culture across a global context, connect corporate values with communities in need and generate measurable business results, all while creating an indelible impact on the social landscape.[22]

I had the opportunity of talking with Bryan de Lottinville, the founder and CEO of Benevity, about the company and how he leads it. When I asked Bryan to give me some history on why he started the company, he told me that he wished the story was more glamorous. He had been a lawyer in a previous life and, as a partner in a large law firm in Toronto, he had worked on financing for growth companies. He left in the mid-nineties to take an operational role in a company that grew from approximately $20 million to $300 million in revenue over his six-year tenure. After selling this company to a large US firm, he left to run iStockphoto, one of the first multi-sided businesses that involved user-generated content, crowdsourcing, and a broad community to achieve a network effect in the stock imagery business. He described iStock as very disruptive. The company grew quickly and the owners sold it. This was Bryan's first foray into technology. Around this time, his young daughter asked him what he did for a living. His immediate answer was that "he fixes up companies and sells them for as much as he can," although that wasn't quite the way he expressed it. Her question, and his own answer, prompted deep reflection. He realized that his actions and his intentions weren't as aligned as he would have liked. He had always intended to leave the world a little better than he found it but, up to that point, those intentions hadn't resulted in much more than writing the occasional check to charity, attending charitable events, and other relatively superficial activities. He told me that he wanted to leave a different legacy.

It was around this time that Bryan began to learn more about the landscape of charitable giving. He was surprised to find that online giving accounted for a very small percentage of charitable donations. Also, he discovered that, for many years, the percentage of overall charitable giving contributed by corporations had remained flat at five percent of the total charitable contributions – even while stakeholder expectations for corporate social responsibility were growing. He attributed this discrepancy to activities that were more hand-out focused than engagement-focused. He told me that when he started to explore the existing space, he found that "the bar was appallingly low" in terms of what was out there. The capabilities that were being offered to corporations were rudimentary and grounded in a fundraising focus rather than in engagement and passion-evoking mentalities. He thought that companies were defining their charitable-giving process far too narrowly and there was an opportunity "to expand the notion beyond the once a year arm-twisting exercise around fundraising by tapping into that human yearning for sense of purpose, meaning and impact." As a step in this direction, he envisioned a user-centric platform for individuals within companies to make their own decisions about how to allocate their charitable dollars. His goal for the longer term is for Benevity to act as a catalyst to infuse a culture of "goodness" into the world. He believes that by helping companies enable people to bring their best selves to work, a culture of meaning and purpose will be created that will help companies produce more business and social impact. That is why he started Benevity.

When I asked Bryan how companies can inspire employees to sign-on to a vision, he replied that first leaders must have a vision! And they must be authentically committed to it. The vision should be resonant, relatable, and aspirational. People need to feel an emotional connection to it if the vision is to come alive throughout the company.

Bryan argues that the top-level leaders have a responsibility to engage people with the vision and invest in a positive culture. However, he maintains that culture is never created completely through top-down efforts. In Bryan's words, culture must be "democratized both horizontally and vertically." He maintains that a corporate culture is composed of a thousand little things, including the language that is used, the attributes and values that are recruited for and promoted, and what gets recognized and rewarded. Rather than providing common rewards such as trinkets and other perks, Benevity offers social incentives. For example, Benevity uses its own software to match employees' charitable donations, to reward employee volunteering by giving money to a charity of the employee's choice through a "Dollars for Doers" program, and deposits donation currency in employees' "giving accounts" as a reward for other targeted behaviors. Benevity believes in using prosocial rewards to honor prosocial behavior.

Bryan de Lottinville wants to change the world for the better. To that end, he explains that Benevity is attempting to create agents of change by engaging people in good acts around meaning and purpose within companies. He believes that changing the world comes from culture change. He emphasizes that a leader can inspire but that everyone in the organization contributes to culture.

Benevity's reputation along with their phenomenal growth supports de Lottinville's vision. While he is proud of Benevity's B Corporation status, his hope is that, someday, the special status will be unnecessary, in that every company will integrate for-profit goals with social impact.

Moving towards a sustainable culture

The process of creating and supporting a sustainable internal organizational culture includes several actions such as those that follow.

Communicate an inspiring vision that is shared

Engagement is strongest in the workplace when a leader's vision is so powerful that it touches the emotions and imaginations of employees. In the article "To Lead, Create a Shared Vision," authors James Kouzes and Barry Posner report on a study of thousands of people who responded to the question, "What do you look for and admire in a leader?"[23] Seventy-two percent said that they want a leader who is forward-looking. However, they also said that they want the leaders' visions to reflect their own desires and values. In other words, people are looking for leaders who can create and facilitate a vision that is shared across the organization. The authors conclude that "The only visions that take hold are shared visions—and you will create them only when you listen very, very closely to others, appreciate their hopes, and attend to their needs."

Align words and deeds

While leaders' inspirational visions that incorporate workforce desires and values get the attention of employees, their actions must match their words. Instead of merely signing on to the vision, employees look for evidence of true company commitment. They listen for the rationale, look for how the company promises to integrate the vision with decision-making, and watch what leaders do in addition to what they say. The adage "actions speak louder than words" holds up. If the leaders' actions are inconsistent with their expressed commitments, employees are skeptical at best and quite possibly cynical about the vision. A participant in one of our studies said the following:

> There is a difference between presenting a clear vision to someone at my level and actually having a clear vision that drives your decisions. I know that long-term sustainability goals have been clearly stated, but I don't know how often a short-term profit has been passed up because of true belief in those goals. I have based my responses on actions that I have seen or heard of, not on top down communications that I am not able to validate.

This comment represents many similar opinions expressed by the employees of this company. Interestingly, the company has a sterling reputation for its work in sustainability. Yet many employees expressed skepticism about the authenticity of the commitments. Even though the company leaders communicated a vision, the employees told us they did not believe that the vision was taken seriously. They doubted the true commitment of their leaders to it. Based on many similar comments, we might conclude that the trustworthiness of the leaders was in doubt. And trustworthiness of leaders has a strong influence on engagement.

Embed the vision and commitments into the organization

Make company purpose and commitments more than a set of initiatives that run parallel to the real work. Instead, make it the real work! The following quote is from an employee of a sustainable company with a sustainable culture: "In our company sustainability is a mindset and not a problem to be solved. Our company has a vision of how to win and our commitment to our purpose is foundational to the strategy."

Connect employees' work with the vision

Ensure that employees understand how their work connects to the company purpose and vision. Recently we conducted an informal survey concerning employee engagement and sustainability. Almost all of the 101 people (92 percent) who responded said that learning more about sustainability was important to them. Yet fewer than half (42 percent) said that they were highly engaged in their companies' sustainability efforts. Companies have a long way to go in embedding their purpose and commitments into the day-to-day work of everyone throughout the entire organization. When asked about how their purpose-driven company could improve, an employee told us the following: "Have alignment on the annual vision/goals in an EXECUTABLE manner, from the top down. Identify clear priorities in our day-to-day jobs so that we can prioritize the tasks that contribute most towards Company's goals."

Remember that engagement follows purpose

Over the years, we have heard the hopes and dreams of many people in the workforce. They have told us about what inspires them in their own work. A statement from a participant in our most recent study sums up what we have heard for a decade: "It is inspiring to be working with this company to make the world a better place! I work harder and try to resolve things more effectively because I work with a company that has such a strong social mission."

People thrive in organizations where the purpose beyond profit is evident and all share a common vision.

Case: from purpose, to participation, to engagement

Early in my career I had the opportunity of experiencing first-hand what a truly purpose-driven, engaged workforce looks like. I was hired by a company in the specialty chemical industry to create a more effective operator training program to support the organization's purpose and vision. While the company was firmly committed to financial success and to meeting the expectations of their shareholders, they were also dedicated to the growth and development of *all* employees, and to organizing work to best draw on their knowledge and skills. In the words of the plant manager,

> The way I see it, we are just going to have to get better at everything. To be competitive, we must treat employees as more than just a pair of hands. We want to compete with brains. And we must reorganize work so that everyone is involved with our vision and shares responsibility for contributing to our culture. What good are skills if you don't allow people to use them?

From my first day working with this company to my last, I realized that this organization functioned with a different culture than most. They believed that the best performance came from a workplace where all employees were empowered to use their intellect. To this end they demonstrated their commitment to replacing the more traditional command and control hierarchy with a system where all employees were involved in decisions that affected their work. They created work designs that allowed for high levels of autonomy and a focus on work teams, many of which were self-directed. Never before and never since have I experienced a culture that was as clearly grounded in respect for the dignity of every employee and a level of professionalism that was evident across the entire organization. Across the board people were committed to each other, their company, and their teams, and showed a level of energy and engagement that I had not seen before. My experiences with this company were by far the best of my career. It is through this work that I became a true believer that passion follows purpose. If you want your employees to engage, give them a reason to believe.

Summary and conclusions

Sustainable companies have unique internal cultures. Company purpose is evident to employees who see their leaders commit to it personally. Leaders in sustainable companies have a strategy for engaging employees in the vision. They encourage continuous learning which supports their emphasis on innovation.

Because the purpose and other aspects of the company identity are embedded into business plans, processes, and policies, employees understand how their work connects with it and they find meaning in it as a result. Employees believe that their contribution is appreciated, and they feel valued. The greater their belief that sustainability is crucial to the company's future the more they engage.

Your turn: assessing engagement

Step 1: What does your company do to engage employees in an inspiring vision? Reflect on the questions in the table below and jot down your thoughts.

Engagement in your company	Your thoughts
What is your company's approach/strategy for engaging employees in the vision?	
How engaged are employees, in general, in your company?	
To what degree do employees in your company understand how their own work connects with the company purpose? What could you and others in the company do to improve these connections?	

Step 2: Think about your own area of influence and reflect on the questions in the table below.

Engagement in your area of influence	Your thoughts
How engaged are the people on your own team or in your area of influence?	
Do people in your area of influence understand how their work connects with the overall vision and purpose of the team/department/area? What could you do to improve these connections?	

Notes

1 Steve Jobs quotes. *BrainyQuote.com*, BrainyMedia Inc., 2018, accessed November 1, 2018. Available at: www.brainyquote.com/quotes/steve_jobs_416859.
2 P&G website accessed September 15, 2018. Available at: https://news.pg.com/press-release/pg-corporate-announcements/pg-named-one-americas-best-corporate-citizens.
3 *P&G 2017 Citizenship Report*, accessed September 15, 2018. Available at: https://assets.ctfassets.net/oggad6svuzkv/3zpnn3xyOAAQIeMSgqs2K2/cbdc982f-7b7ae4d9f3346dc866dcccc7/2017_Citizenship_Report_Executive_Summary.pdf.
4 "Working at P&G," website accessed September 15, 2018. Available at: www.pgcareers.com.
5 *P&G 2017 Citizenship Report Executive Summary*, accessed November 6, 2018. Available at:www.pg.com/fr_FR/downloads/sustainability/2017_PG_Citizenship_Report_executive_summary.pdf.
6 "P&G 2016 Citizenship Report Executive Summary," Accessed on November 6, 2018. Available at: https://us.pg.com/citizenship-example/citizenship-report/sustainability-reports.
7 *The Employee Experience Index Around the Globe: How Countries Measure Up and Create Human Workplaces*, IBM Corporation ("IBM") and Globoforce Limited ("Globoforce") 2017, 6. Available at: https://resources.globoforce.com/research-reports/employee-experience-around-the-globe#.
8 Kelly Pledger Weeks, "Every Generation Wants Meaningful Work – But Thinks Other Age Groups are in it for the Money," *Harvard Business Review*, July 31, 2017. Available at: https://hbr.org/2017/07/every-generation-wants-meaningful-work-but-thinks-other-age-groups-are-in-it-for-the-money.
9 Theresa Amabile and Scott Kramer, "Inner Work Life: The Hidden Subtext of Business Performance," *Harvard Business Review*, (May 2007), 85, no. 5, 72–83.

10 Theresa Amabile and Scott Kramer, *The Progress Principle: Optimizing Inner Work Life to Create Value*, (Harvard Business Review Press, 2012).

11 "The State of Employee Engagement, 2018," *HR.com*, sponsored by GLINT, whitepaper accessed on website, October 1, 2018. Available at: www.glintinc.com/resource/the-state-of-employee-engagement-in-2018.

12 "Employee Engagement," *Wikipedia*, accessed October 1, 2018. Available at: https://en.wikipedia.org/wiki/Employee_engagement.

13 "Gallup Workplace," *Gallup*, accessed October 4, 2018. Available at: www.gallup.com/workplace/229424/employee-engagement.aspx?g_source=link_wwwv9&g_campaign=item_237437&g_medium=copy.

14 *Driving Performance and Retention Through Employee Engagement*, Corporate Leadership Council of the Corporate Executive Board, 2004, accessed October 3, 2018. Available at: http://cwfl.usc.edu/assets/pdf/Employee%20engagement.pdf.

15 Catherine Bailey, Adrian Madden, Kerstin Alfes, and Luke Fletcher, "The Meaning, Antecedents and Outcomes of Employee Engagement: A Narrative Evidence Synthesis," *International Journal of Management Reviews*, (2015), 19, no. 1, 31–53, ISSN 1460-8545. Available at: http://sro.sussex.ac.uk/54474/1/IJMR_Engagement_Synthesis_third_submission.pdf.

16 "Engaged Employees Less Likely to Have Health Problems," *Gallup*, December 15, 2015, accessed October 1, 2018. Available at: https://news.gallup.com/poll/187865/engaged-employees-less-likely-health-problems.aspx.

17 "The Right Culture: Not Just About Employee Satisfaction," *Gallup*, April 12, 2017. Accessed October 5, 2018. https://www.gallup.com/workplace/236366/right-culture-not-employee-satisfaction.aspx

18 Susan Sorenson, "Employee Engagement Drives Growth," *Workplace*, June 2013. Available at: www.gallup.com/workplace/236927/employee-engagement-drives-growth.aspx.

19 "The Engaged Workplace," *Gallup*, accessed October 1, 2018. Available at: https://news.gallup.com/poll/165269/worldwide-employees-engaged-work.aspx.

20 "State of Employee Engagement, 2018," *HR.com*, sponsored by GLINT. Available at: www.glintinc.com/resource/the-state-of-employee-engagement-in-2018.

21 "State of the Workplace 2017," *Gallup*, 2017, 9. Available at: www.workflexibility.org/report-summary-state-american-workplace-gallup-2017.

22 Benevity website. Accessed on September 5, 2018. Available at: www.benevity.com.

23 James Kouzes and Barry Posner, "To Lead, Create a Shared Vision," *Harvard Business Review*, January, 2009. Available at: https://hbr.org/2009/01/to-lead-create-a-shared-vision.

6 External relationships

Embracing the unusual suspects

Chapter purpose

Yogi Berra once said, "The future ain't what it used to be." Likewise, it could be said that organizational boundaries aren't what they once were. We all have external stakeholders, meaning persons and groups interested in our companies. And our relationships with our stakeholders are changing. Sustainable companies interact and collaborate more with external stakeholders, and send clear and consistent messages to them about their purpose, vision, and commitments. They care more about their reputation with the public, and, therefore, work to become trustworthy.

The purpose of this chapter is to examine the relationships of people and companies with others outside of their own corporate boundaries. This chapter will explore how stakeholders can affect all companies and why sustainable companies are more engaged with them. It will provide you with tips for successfully collaborating with others outside your own organization.

Twenty-first-century approach to external stakeholders

Our views of organizational boundaries have changed over the last decade. Formerly, solid lines separated our companies from the rest of the world. Often, we viewed the people, organizations, and institutions on the other side of the line with suspicion. However, now boundaries are more fluid. Organizations are collaborating with others for many reasons, including tackling societal problems that require varying expertise and perspectives.

Our own research shows that the top-level leaders of sustainable companies are often inspired by people external to their own organizational boundaries. As they learn from others, they actively encourage their employees to do the same.

Who are the most critical stakeholders?

All companies, no matter what industry or size, have numerous stakeholders, meaning people or groups interested in or affected by them. Stakeholders include, among others, customers, employees, investors, and communities.

Most of us recognize that no matter whether they take an arm's length interest or interact with our companies directly, our stakeholders do have the capability of influencing our organizations' futures. In the words of Rob Frederick, V.P. and Director of Corporate Responsibility at Brown-Forman, one of the largest American-owned companies in the spirits and wine industry, therefore "we embrace the *unusual* suspects."[1]

Some have estimated that companies have up to 20 stakeholder groups that can influence their outcomes in one way or another.[2] Since companies can't respond to all stakeholders' requests and concerns, most set priorities around the groups they consider to be most likely to have an impact on the performance of the company. Subsequently they gather input on the issues that are most significant to their high-priority stakeholders, followed by an assessment of which issues are most important to their own interests. This analysis helps companies determine where to place their resources and what to measure and report on annually.

While the results of this process, sometimes referred to as materiality analysis, varies, we have identified several stakeholder groups that tend to show up on many, if not most, companies' radars: Customers, communities, and investors.

Customers

All companies consider their customers to be significant stakeholders. Some companies sell to consumers – a process I will refer to as B2C. Others market their products and services to businesses, or B2B. And some sell to both.

Business and conscious consumers (B2C)

Consumer activism is on the rise. Consumers are showing an increasing interest in brand ethics specifically related to the environment and other societal challenges. More specifically, they want to know whether companies/brands follow through on their promises regarding social responsibility. A recent global survey showed that 77 percent of consumers prefer to buy from companies that are responsible to their communities. And they are willing to pay 5 to 10 percent more for their products and services.[3] This report uses the term "conscious consumers" to describe those who consider company ethics and track records in addressing environmental and social issues when making buying decisions. Since 74 percent of the conscious consumers said that they actively comment on brands through social media, most likely this group has a significant impact on brand reputation. Of course, companies must do more than merely claim to be socially responsible. They must also demonstrate their contribution to society.

Case: Procter and Gamble's purpose in action

David Taylor, CEO and Chairman of the Board of consumer goods giant Procter and Gamble, states on their website that P&G lives its purpose and values through their citizenship efforts. Their commitments are built into the way they achieve business results. You will recall that I discussed their areas of focus in the last chapter, including: community impact, diversity and inclusion, gender equality, and environmental responsibility. They chose gender equality as a focus because many of their customers are women. Thus, this cause is clearly connected to their business. They believe that their insights into the lives, aspirations, and challenges of females enable them to be strong advocates for change. They are carrying out their commitments by leveraging their voice in media and advertising, removing barriers to education and economic opportunities, and striving to achieve 50/50 representation of women and men in their own company.[4]

Procter and Gamble has produced a series of videos, including the #LikeAGirl and #WeSeeEqual ads, to carry their campaign forward. Anyone who has viewed the videos will recognize the emotional impact. Over time, the campaigns are likely to have a positive effect on their business as well as on consumers who share the P&G values for gender equality.

Business to business (B2B)

Businesses whose customers are consumers (B2C) aren't the only ones to benefit from articulating their values. These days very few companies can carry out a purpose and achieve sustainability outcomes without demanding the same from their suppliers. Therefore, business buyers are closely examining how their vendors address environmental and social responsibility. Sustainable companies, more than others, encourage their suppliers to commit to sustainability.

Companies with aggressive sustainability objectives understand that the actions of their suppliers contribute to whether they can meet their goals. In fact, many companies have found that their supply chain offers the greatest opportunity for reducing their environmental impact and increasing social impact. In fact, the U.S. government's Environmental Protection Agency (EPA) reported that in many industries approximately 75 percent of a company's greenhouse gas emissions come from its supply chain rather than from direct operations.[5] When companies calculate their environmental footprint, most find that they are implicitly, if not explicitly, reporting on the aggregate footprint of their suppliers. Therefore, many are asking their suppliers to track and report their own progress on sustainability-related goals.

Some companies not only ask their suppliers to track but also to reduce their carbon emissions and other environmental impacts. A growing number of companies are signing on to The Carbon Disclosure Project (CDP), a program established to enable companies and their supply chains to collaborate in identifying and managing climate change, water usage, and deforestation. Nevertheless, CDP's 2018 report stated that while over three quarters of suppliers responding to their standardized reporting system identified some inherent climate change risks, just over half (52 percent) said that they had integrated climate change into their business strategy. The CDP report concluded that there are many missed opportunities to impact climate change while cutting costs at the same time.[6]

A company's suppliers can positively affect their customers' environmental and social sustainability records and reputations in many ways. For example, in 1996, Nike experienced damage to its reputation because of child labor practices in factories comprising their supply chain. Nike addressed the issues relatively quickly. However, the company's reputation didn't truly begin to mend until the mid-2000s when Nike began pulling its products from suppliers that didn't meet decent working standards. Over time Nike has become recognized as a leader in tackling sustainability-related issues in its supply chain.[7]

As companies continue to recognize how their suppliers can influence their ability to become sustainable, expectations are rising. Businesses selling to other businesses are unique in that, typically, they have far fewer potential customers than businesses selling to consumers and the magnitude of the purchases is greater. Thus, businesses selling to other businesses can strengthen their relationships with valuable customers – or potential customers – by understanding and supporting their sustainability objectives through their own commitments and actions. As a result, companies can become more socially responsible, while also cutting costs and generating and retaining customers in the B2B world.

A growing number of organizations and industries are working together to support their value chains and to track their performance in areas related to sustainability.

Examples

- Walmart has been applying a sustainability index to evaluate their product suppliers' performance for many years. In 2016, they launched Project Gigaton which targeted the reduction of emissions in their supply chain by one gigaton (one billion metric tons) by the year 2030. They invited their suppliers to enter in to the project. To participate, suppliers must set emissions reduction targets and report their progress annually. In return, they are eligible for recognition opportunities.[8]
- The aluminum industry has instituted a global certification process administered by a non-profit standards organization, The Aluminum Stewardship Initiative (ASI). This initiative is a result of producers, users, and stakeholders in the aluminum industry committing to maximizing the contribution of the aluminum industry to a sustainable society. The mission of the ASI is to recognize and collaboratively foster responsible production, sourcing, and stewardship of aluminum. The ASI developed Chain of Custody (CoC) Certification to support businesses in the aluminum value chain that wish to provide their customers and stakeholders with independent assurance for responsible production and sourcing of aluminum.[9]

- The Food and Agriculture Organization of the United Nations has created a Sustainable Food Value Chain (SFVC) framework. The framework describes the food value chain as "a complex system of economic, social and natural environments that determine the behavior and performance of farms and other agri-food enterprises."[10] They define the food value chain as all who are involved in the coordinated activities needed to produce food. Their goal is to increase the knowledge needed by members of the value chain to become more sustainable. Over the years several food-related value chain certifications have launched. For example, the Rain Forest Alliance certifies stakeholders in the coffee value chain through an assessment of environmental, social, and economic criteria targeted towards protecting biodiversity, contributing to respect for workers and local communities, and delivering financial benefits to farmers.[11] Likewise, UTZ certifies both farms and corporations based on sustainability-related standards. In 2017 UTZ and the Rain Forest Alliance merged. The combined organization plans to create a new certification process which will draw from the best practices in each of their individual programs.[12]

These examples are among many collaborative initiatives aimed at setting sustainability-related standards for stakeholders in a value chain and providing them with support for meeting the expectations of their customers and consumers.

Local community

All our companies are located within communities. And our neighbors have a stake in how we conduct our business. Companies that pollute the air or contaminate the water run the risk of losing their communities' acceptance.

Your company can establish acceptance – often referred to as a license to operate – by being a good corporate citizen. Avoiding negative impacts on the community is a good start. However, to truly earn your social license to operate you must also give back to the community.

According to a recent report issued by the Network for Business Sustainability, establishing good relations with communities helps companies in several ways. They suggest the following benefits:

- First, when your company considers community concerns, you are likely to make better decisions.
- Second, two-way communications between your company and the community builds trust.
- Third, good community relations will increase your company's competitiveness by making it easier for you to attract workers.
- Obstacles that can affect your company's productivity and viability, such as the threat of lawsuits, are likely to become less problematic.

The report proposes that companies work with communities in three ways:

1   Investment: Giving back – the company provides resources to the community.
2   Involvement: Building bridges – the company uses input from the community to shape its actions.
3   Integration: Changing society – the company and the community jointly manage projects.[13]

Case: collective impact for communities

In 2006 over 300 local organizations, including corporations, in the Cincinnati, Ohio, and Northern Kentucky area came together to use their collective resources and expertise to improve education in the region. They referred to the team as the Strive Partnership. Together they created a shared agenda to leverage existing programs towards shared goals. And they used shared measurement systems to track progress. Over a ten-year time period, 86 percent of the student outcome indicators in the region have improved.[14] This approach to tackling community issues became known as collective impact. Strive is one of many initiatives that demonstrate the power of companies partnering with others in the community to change society.

Investors and shareholders

Those of us with investors and shareholders understand that they are critical to our businesses since they provide financing. In this age of activists, it behooves companies to understand investors' and shareholders' priorities.

A 2016 study sponsored by the *MIT Sloan Management Review* and Boston Consulting[15] showed that investors care more about sustainability than the company executives think. Because investors connect a company's sustainability performance to its financial performance they are using sustainability data as input to their decisions. In addition, socially responsible investment funds enabling impact investing are on the rise. These trends mean that companies should be paying more attention to investors' priorities.

Consider again Larry Fink's annual letter to CEOs in 2018. Fink, the CEO of Blackrock, the global investment management corporation, suggested that companies should engage with their shareholders about how they can improve their long-term value by investing in innovation, employee development, and other things that build long-term growth.[16]

Impact investing is a growing industry according to the nonprofit organization The Global Impact Investing Network (GIIN). They state that "Impact investments are investments made into companies, organizations, and funds with the intention to generate social and environmental impact alongside a financial return." The GIIN conducts a survey of impact investors annually. In 2018, they surveyed 229 of the world's largest impact investing organizations including fund managers, banks, foundations, pension funds, and insurance companies, among others. They reported that collectively they manage over $228 billion USD in impact investing assets. And they noted that the number of new investors has grown substantially over the past decade. Over the past year, they have seen the entry of many well-known large-scale firms. The GIIN concludes that the annual survey shows momentum for the impact investing market. However, more importantly, they believe that they are seeing a shift in broader financial markets. They suggest that it is becoming unacceptable in mainstream markets to ignore social and environmental impacts of investments. The Research Director, Abhilash Mudaliar, states "Fundamental norms governing the role and purpose of capital in society are changing, and impact investing is at the forefront driving this transformational shift."[17]

Engaging with externals

As you can see from the examples in the previous section, companies engage with people and organizations outside of their own boundaries for a variety of reasons. Sometimes, companies strive to form relationships with stakeholder groups to burnish their reputations. Some reach out to better understand their needs, interests, and concerns. The most sustainable companies look outward to identify the societal problems that they are positioned to address. As I mentioned in Chapter 4, engagement with those outside our boundaries must be built on trust.

Tips for engaging with externals: how to build trust

Becoming trustworthy in the eyes of our external stakeholders takes time and effort. It is more than a public relations initiative. It goes beyond what we write on our websites and sell as our brand. We must be authentic and transparent. I offer the following recommendations for building strong relationships with external stakeholders.

Avoid corporate spin

We can harm our trustworthiness through corporate "spin." A 2016 study conducted by Bain and Company showed that only 2 percent of the companies they surveyed achieved their sustainability goals. They found several reasons for the failure. However, one of the most telling is that 62 percent of the respondents said that their companies set the goals in the first place only for their public reputation.[18] Stakeholders will recognize this kind of corporate spin sooner or later. And, when spotted, corporate spin erodes trust.

Communicate authentically and transparently

Trust grows with authentic communications and interactions with others. If we are more concerned with telling our story than having a story to tell, we are failing to give our customers, investors, communities, and the public a reason to believe in us.

Ensure that actions match messages

Companies earn the trust of their stakeholders over time. While identifying a purpose and communicating it widely can be good, how we behave considering that purpose is more important. When companies tout their philanthropy in the community while polluting the air and water, or when they only report their successes with sustainability while covering up their failures, they are likely to receive well-deserved scorn rather than trust from the public.

Collaborating with externals

While many companies reach out for more than one reason, all of which are legitimate, I would like to turn to the relationships that move beyond engagement to collaboration. Many companies, especially the most sustainable, reach outside their own boundaries to collaborate with other organizations. At times they do so to complement their own expertise as they tackle complex problems that require many types of knowledge and skill. Other times, they join with others to extend their reach or to expand their clout in addressing issues of mutual concern.

Complementing own expertise and perspectives

Some companies form alliances with unusual partners such as NGOs to complement their own expertise and perspectives. Consider, for example, the companies that participate in the value chain alliances I described earlier in this chapter, such as the Rain Forest Alliance. The members of these alliances are collaborating to tackle problems that no one organization could solve on its own.

Likewise, the Nature Conservancy and Dow created an alliance back in 2011 to integrate the value of nature into business decisions. They maintained that this integration would lead to both better business results and more desirable conservation outcomes. Their 2016 progress report showed how reforestation can serve as a business solution to improve air quality. In addition, the report addressed how to mitigate risks of water shortages, and how to use nature as an asset to protect business infrastructure.[19] Currently Dow is working towards incorporating nature into business decisions in all aspects of their company. For example, the alliance developed a tool for assessing the value of ecosystem services. Dow set a goal of using the tool, which they labeled Nature's Future Value, for all their real estate and capital projects by 2020.[20]

Leaders of socially responsible companies, such as Interface, the sustainable modular carpet company, approach their work from a holistic, systems perspective. Their website states,

Interconnectedness is at the heart of all we do. After all, the genius of our product comes alive when carpet tiles connect into a beautiful, functional mosaic. We came to see our company that way too – one part of a broader picture – and that transformed us. Now, we understand the world in terms of systems, an intricate web of dependencies, and we think in partnerships, knowing none of us is as smart as all of us. Through collaboration with each other, design leadership and world-shaping visionaries, we do great things, together.[21]

Extend reach and expand clout

Even companies that compete in some areas are working together in others for their mutual benefit. A new term has been applied to this balancing between cooperation and competition – cooptition.[22] For example, BMW and Toyota are collaborating to create a hybrid sports car that each will sell under its own brand.[23] Refrigerants, Naturally! with members such as the Coca-Cola company and PepsiCo, is a global initiative exploring innovations in cooling technologies that are natural and more climate-friendly. Many of the international participants are direct competitors.[24] The International Federation of Pharmaceutical Manufacturers and Associations (IFPMA) was formed to find ways to curb antimicrobial resistance that causes drug-resistant infections.[25] The motivations for these collaborations vary. However, almost all aim to expand their expertise and areas of influence and to address mutual concerns.

Collaboration among smaller firms

These cross-boundary partnerships are not just for large multinational companies. Even smaller firms are partnering with others for a variety of reasons. Some seek out new relationships to reach a larger market. Others join to exploit complementary expertise. And more than a few collaborate to achieve the collective impact that I discussed previously. While some of these relationships are more structured than others, all are held together by webs of mutual expectations and the belief that each party offers value to the collaborative community.

Case: collaborating for collective impact

Canopy is a nonprofit organization that serves as a network for good businesses in Kentucky. Located in Louisville, most of its members are small and mid-size businesses. The aim is to leverage the potential and capabilities of these socially responsible small and mid-size businesses for positive, measurable impact and to create meaningful relationships among for-profit/nonprofit and public/private entities to make lives better throughout the state. Their website states, "Canopy will provide the tools and support so that socially-responsible companies, entrepreneurs, and communities can reach their fullest human potential." The strategy is to:

1 Educate – creating demand with consumers for doing business with social enterprises.
2 Facilitate sharing of business models – helping network members learn from each other.
3 Encourage collective impact – encourage these businesses to work together to tackle some of Kentucky's toughest social problems.

The group is developing a third-party certification process for social enterprises in Kentucky. Focusing specifically on areas of impact in Kentucky, the idea is to make the process more localized, accessible, and less expensive than those currently available nationally and internationally. To become certified, companies must commit to transparency and fairness, measure their impact, either internal or social impact, or both, and commit to and track their improvements over time. This certification will enable social enterprises to signal their commitment to social mission. Scott Koloms, the founder of Canopy, says that the long-term goal is to build a robust network of social enterprises and to enhance Kentucky's reputation for attracting these businesses.

Case: collaborating to support each other

The newly minted social enterprise Certifiably is a for-profit enterprise with the goal of making it easier for businesses to find and do business with other companies that share their values, according to founder Anne Chambers. Certifiably is an on-line platform for certified companies, including but not limited to B Corps, Women Owned Businesses (WBE), Minority Owned Businesses (MBE), LGBTQ, Veteran Owned companies, Organic, Fair Trade, and LEED Certified. The platform will allow purchases to be tracked against the United Nations 17 Sustainable Development Goals. So, for example, if a company needs to buy new plastic containers for something like yogurt, the person making the purchase decision will be able to select the types of certified companies they want to work with and dig deeper to see what impact among the 17 SDGs each of those companies is addressing.

Tips for collaborating with externals: how to engage in courageous collaboration

My own small consulting company has partnered with engineering firms, architect and design companies, and energy management organizations to provide clients with services that none of us could have offered alone. I can tell you from first-hand experience that these cross-boundary collaborations can be tricky. When organizations choose to work together, they bring their own cultures, values, and needs. Differing and often hidden assumptions can lead the collaborators into unforeseen traps. If the differences aren't recognized and discussed, cooperation may break down at the most inconvenient times. The best approach to these associations is to plan up-front. The partners should have clear goals and explicit agreements about who is going to do what. And they require each participant to balance self-interest with common interests. Collaboration succeeds only if everyone involved benefits.

Nevertheless, collaborating with other organizations can be very rewarding and often the only way to meet goals. Working together across organizational boundaries is often imperative for finding solutions to the complex problems that we face as we work towards a more sustainable world. No one organization or sector is likely to have enough insight and expertise to make much progress in isolation. It is in all our best interests to learn skills for collaborating and to muster the courage to engage with the "unusual suspects." Recently I ran across a book depicting the life of Ray Kroc, founder of McDonalds. The title of the book is *None of Us is as Good as All of Us*.[26] I believe that this phrase sums up why collaboration is so critical in these challenging times.

Of course, organizations have varied perspectives about the most pressing societal issues. However, within the right conditions, those differences can enhance rather than detract from problem-solving. When distinct groups band together to confront common problems, one-plus-one can equal more than two!

The term "courageous collaboration" was first used by the national non-profit Center for Ethical Leadership. They outlined the qualities that foster courageous collaborations such as establishing trusting relationships, taking risks that matter, and being open to collective creativity.[27] I would like to add to the list.

Reframe: from enemies to partners

To build trust and work collaboratively, organizations must give up the all too prevalent tendencies to view "other" groups as the enemy. For example, government agencies and corporations have viewed their relationships as adversarial from time to time. This view usually includes the assumptions that governments set regulations, corporations seek to work around them, and NGOs attempt to expose them. However, courageous collaboration requires a change in these assumptions. Tackling global problems requires organizations to band together in new types of relationships. The Paris Climate Conference held in 2015 marked the first official recognition that the government cannot solve sustainability-related challenges alone. To succeed in establishing boundary-crossing collectives, organizations must view the others as trusted colleagues and acknowledge that all have a valuable role to play. Only within a trusting environment can collaborative groups achieve what none can accomplish alone.

Avoid acting only from self-interest

If we enter into a collaborative relationship to assure that our self-interests are achieved, we are violating the most important quality of courageous collaborations: Trust. Many times, competitors within the same industry come together to address issues that could affect all. When the members approach these collectives to safeguard their own interests, or to ensure that they prevail over their competitors, creative approaches to shared concerns are unlikely to emerge.

Establish the rules of engagement

All organizations need some certainty to move forward smartly, according to Elizabeth Heider, Chief Sustainability Officer of Skanska USA. She suggested that the varying partners in a collective are likely to have their own disparate rules. Therefore, the members of the groups, whether representing corporations, government, NGOs, universities, or any other organizational type, should establish a common rulebook and sincerely commit to it.[28]

Develop a common language

When the members of a collaborative group come together from dissimilar organizations representing different sectors, industries, or countries, misunderstandings are likely. Only when the members work to understand the perspectives of the others can these confusions be avoided. Heider said that when groups are talking about sustainability-related issues, shared metrics can enable clearer communications. Courageous collaborators can avoid often dooming mix-ups by taking the time to develop a common language.

Summary and conclusions

External stakeholders have strong and clear expectations for our companies now more than ever. And the most common external stakeholder groups, such as customers, communities, and investors, want us to consider more than merely our own self-interest as we conduct our business. They are asking us to pursue a purpose beyond profits. Sustainable businesses are meeting these expectations. To do so, companies are interacting with others outside of their own organizational boundaries like never before. However, in order for these cross-boundary interactions and relationships to be fruitful, we must establish trust that comes from authenticity and transparency. We must avoid trust-eroding corporate spin. Our actions should support our words.

In addition to reaching out to external stakeholders, many companies are entering collaborative relationships that cross boundaries. These courageous collaborations are necessary if we are to solve our many difficult challenges. We can join with others with perspectives and knowledge different from our own to reach common goals. However, the mere existence of a group committed to working together on common challenges isn't enough to guarantee creative solutions. If we truly want to achieve successes that exemplify how one plus one can be greater than two, we will need to rethink some of the assumptions that enable our comfort.

Our colleague and team member Geoff Powter discussed the essential components for collaboration as follows:

To function best, teams need the right people, brought together for the right reasons, at the right time, with the right supports in place. That support is needed because natural problems of communication and coordination within groups can get in the way of best intentions. Teams need a clear purpose, with defined boundaries and roles.[29]

Your turn: assessing external relationships

Is your company trustworthy?

Where does your company stand in the eyes of the public? Reflect on the questions related to trustworthiness and jot down your thoughts in the right-hand column of the table below. If you do not know how the public, your customers, suppliers, or other stakeholders view your company, take the time to gather their input. Your stakeholders' opinions will have a critical impact on your success and most likely your survival as a company.

Do you think that the public views your company as trustworthy? How about your customers? Suppliers? Why or why not? How do you know?	
Do you share your commitments to sustainability with the public? If so, how?	
Are you transparent with your stakeholders when you fall short of your sustainability goals?	

How does your company relate to stakeholders?

Step 1: List the people/groups/institutions who you consider to be your most critical stakeholders.

Step 2: Describe what makes them critical.

Step 3: Describe your company's current relationship with this stakeholder.

Step 4: Describe the relationship with each stakeholder that you desire.

Critical stakeholder	What makes this stakeholder critical?	Describe your company's relationship with this stakeholder

How would you like to see your company relate to the critical stakeholders?

Critical stakeholder	Desired relationship

Notes

1 Rob Frederick, email exchange with author, August 20, 2018.
2 D.C. Esty and A.S. Winston, "Green to Gold: How Smart Companies Use Environmental Strategy to Innovate, Create Value, and Build Competitive Advantage," (New Haven: Yale University Press, 2006).
3 *In Good Company: The Value of Conscious Consumers*, A Union+Weber Research Report (Zendesk: 2017), accessed on September 9, 2018. Available at: https://zen-marketing-content.s3.amazonaws.com/content/whitepapers/Conscious%20Consumerism.pdf.
4 *Citizenship Report Executive Summary*, P&G, 2017, accessed September 8, 2017. Available at: https://assets.ctfassets.net/oggad6svuzkv/3zpnn3xyOAAQIeMSgqs2K2.
5 *Managing Supply Chain Greenhouse Gas Emissions*, Environmental Protection Agency, December 2010, accessed September 8, 2018. Available at: www.epa.gov/sites/production/files/2015-07/documents/managing_supplychain_ghg.pdf.
6 *Closing the Gap: Scaling Up Sustainable Supply Chains*, CDP Supply Chain Report, 2017–2018, accessed September 8, 2018. Available at: www.cdp.net/en/research/global-reports/global-supply-chain-report-2018.
7 "Nike and Child Labour: How it went from Laggard to Leader," Mallen Baker's Clear Reflection, Respectful Business Blog, February 29, 2016, accessed September 2018. Available at: http://mallenbaker.net/article/clear-reflection/nike-and-child-labour-how-it-went-from-laggard-to-leader.
8 "Project Gigaton," Walmart Sustainability Hub, accessed September 9, 2018. Available at: www.walmartsustainabilityhub.com/project-gigaton.
9 "About ASI," Aluminum Stewardship Initiative, accessed September 9, 2018. Available at: https://aluminium-stewardship.org/about-asi.
10 "Sustainable Food Value Chains Knowledge Platform," Food and Agriculture Organization of the United Nations, accessed September 2018. Available at: www.fao.org/sustainable-food-value-chains/what-is-it/en.
11 "Rain Forest Alliance Certified Coffee," Rain Forest Alliance, accessed September 9, 2018. Available at: www.rainforest-alliance.org/articles/rainforest-alliance-certified-coffee.
12 "New Certification Program," UTZ website, accessed September 9, 2018. Available at: https://utz.org/new-certification-program.
13 "Improving Community Relations," Network for Business Sustainability, November 5, 2012, accessed September 8, 2018. Available at: https://nbs.net/p/improving-community-relations-6b4f4e2d-4625-42fc-99e6-71840f876610-.
14 Strive Impact website, accessed September 8, 2018. Available at: www.strivetogether.org/impact.
15 Gregory Unruh, David Kiroon, Nina Kruschwitz, Martin Reeves, Holger Rubel, and Alexander Meyer Zumfelde, "Investing for a Sustainable Future," *MIT Sloan Management Review*, May 11, 2016, accessed September 8, 2018. Available at: https://sloanreview.mit.edu/projects/investing-for-a-sustainable-future.
16 Larry Fink, *Annual Letter to Shareholders, 2018*. Available at: www.blackrock.com/corporate/investor-relations/larry-fink-chairmans-letter.
17 Abhilash Mudaliar, Rachel Bass, and Hannah Dithrich, *Annual Impact Investor Survey 2018*, Global Impact Investing Network, Sponsors: United States Agency for International Development (USAID) and Department for International Development's Impact Programme (DFID) British Government, accessed September 2018. Available at: https://thegiin.org/research/publication/annualsurvey2018.

18 Jenny Davis-Peccoud, Paul Stone, and Clare Tovey, *Achieving Breakthrough Results in Sustainability*, Bain and Company, 2016. Available at: www.bain.com/contentassets/bd8f5f0eaede4b5db624fb617470aa1b/bain_brief_achieving_breakthrough_results_in_sustainability.pdf.

19 *Working Together to Value Nature, 2016 Summary Report*, The Nature Conservancy and The Dow Chemical Company, accessed September 8, 2018. Available at: www.nature.org/about-us/working-with-companies/companies-we-work-with/dow/2016-collaboration-report.pdf.

20 *2025 Sustainability Goals: Valuing Nature*, Dow Corporate, accessed September 8, 2018. Available at: www.dow.com/en-us/science-and-sustainability/2025-sustainability-goals/valuing-nature.

21 "Interface: Performance with Purpose," accessed September 2, 2018. Available at: www.interface.com/US/en-US/about/mission/Interface-Values-en_US.

22 "Cooptition," definition, *BusinessDictionary.com*, WebFinance Inc., accessed September 3, 2018. Available at: www.businessdictionary.com/definition/cooptition.html.

23 Richard Reeves, "Companies in Coalition: When Enemies Become (Temporary) Friends," *MIT Management Today*, April 22, 2015. Available at: www.managementtoday.co.uk/companies-coalition-when-enemies-become-temporary-friends/article/1343885.

24 Refrigerants, Naturally! website, accessed September 8, 2018. Available at: www.refrigerantsnaturally.com.

25 IFPMA website, accessed September 2018. Available at: www.ifpma.org/resource-centre/new-alliance-to-drive-and-measure-industry-progress-to-curb-antimicrobial- resistance.

26 Patricia Sowell Harris, *None of Us is As Good as All of Us: How McDonalds Prospers by Embracing Inclusion and Diversity* (Wiley, 2009).

27 "What is Courageous Collaboration," Center for Ethical Leadership, 2011. Available at: www.ethicalleadership.org/gs-blog-8/what-is-courageous-collaboration.

28 Elizabeth Heider, personal communication with the author, March 11, 2016.

29 Geoff Powter, personal communication with the author, November 4, 2018.

7 Enhancing change capabilities

Chapter purpose

A few years ago, I was working with a client organization on large-scale change. The leader of the process told me that one of her employees asked when all this change would subside so that she could get back to work. The leader chuckled as she relayed this story to me. Clearly there is no end in sight for changes that will have an impact on our organizations. Change is a constant in our world. Therefore, our capacity for handling it, both at personal and organizational levels, is critical. Our research shows that sustainable companies address change better than others. Why? I believe that the answer lies in their mindsets as well as in the capabilities they have developed and the practices they have adopted that have made them change-adept.

The purpose of this chapter is to explore what makes sustainable companies change-adept and to examine the personal capabilities needed to lead change. While the chapter does not delve into specific approaches to managing change, it does explore the fundamentals of change as they apply to all of us and our companies. The chapter includes some tips for how leaders can prepare to lead change.

Sustainable companies and change

Change can be difficult. And most companies do not have strong track records for even small changes let alone large-scale change. They may be able to develop project plans with specific identifiable steps for moving from one way of doing things to another. However, they are inadequate when it comes to more complex and large-scale change. My research reveals that sustainable companies, when compared with others, have stronger track records with change.

Let's look at some of the unique qualities that may explain their relative success with change.

Living with uncertainty

To become change-adept, organizations must be comfortable moving ahead in the face of uncertainty. Sustainable companies almost always live with uncertainty because they are frequently grappling with challenges that have no quick solutions. Therefore, they experiment, invent, innovate – and these actions are charged with uncertainty.

Uncertainty is a way of life for sustainable companies. They do not look for quick fixes to complex problems. Instead they appreciate that they will not find solutions overnight and they adopt a long-term approach. Since tried and true tactics often fail to address the issues they are tackling, they take more risks than their less sustainable counterparts. Risks hold uncertainty. And they can live with it.

Challenging the status quo

Sustainable companies encourage everyone in the organization to challenge the status quo, a practice that is part of being proactive and anticipating change. Many more traditional companies fail to foster this critical change-related quality. Sometimes they punish people who push against "what we have always done." An employee in one of our less change-adept client organizations told us, "Challenge the status quo and you will be labeled stubborn and not a team player." Yet the companies growing the fastest are disruptors, rejecting the status quo completely. By constantly challenging assumptions, sustainable companies are in a better position to foresee impending changes. And by focusing on innovation, they are in an advantageous position to achieve breakthroughs and significant improvements in products or services.

Reflecting and learning on the job

Sustainable companies encourage continuous learning on the job. In our work with hundreds of organizations, we have encountered very few where people believe that they know how to or have the time to learn while working. Yet sustainable companies do this better than most. They are more likely than others to reward continuous learning, the framework for creating and improving. Toyota Motor Manufacturing offers a great example of an effective approach to learning on the job. Famous for their commitment to continuous improvement, Toyota emphasizes the importance of continuous learning as well. When we worked with them on organizational redesigns, we observed their standard processes for reflection and learning, deeply embedded in the way they do their work. For example, upon completing a project or a phase of it, they reflect on what worked and what didn't. Through reflection they identify the root causes of problems and learn from their mistakes. They adopt what they refer to as counter measures, or new ways to do the work to address the root causes of problems. Toyota and others following the Toyota Production System (TPS) show what it means to have a learning organization.

In addition to learning through reflection, sustainable companies encourage their employees to learn from people and institutions outside of their own boundaries. In fact, this is one of the most consistent and strong differences between sustainable companies and others. Perhaps because of higher levels of trust and transparency, they find it easier to seek out and interact with external stakeholders. They tend to reject the notion that all the knowledge they need resides within their own boundaries. You will recall that this is one reason sustainable companies collaborate with external organizations.

Integrating sustainable strategies with innovation

Our research has shown that one of the greatest differences between sustainable companies and others is how they integrate sustainable strategies with radical innovation.[1] Companies committed to incorporating sustainability into their business strategies have told us that they must innovate because the solutions to the thorny problems that environmental and social challenges present often do not yet exist. Based on stories that we have heard, my colleagues and I have concluded that sustainability serves as a "forcing function" for innovation.[2]

Perhaps sustainable companies are more attuned to the global trends and developments and are poised to apply their capabilities to address what they find. However, rarely can they solve global problems with their existing ways of operating. As our research shows, they commit to innovation as their means for addressing market and societal needs. Also, as I discussed in Chapter 6, they interact more with the "unusual suspects," or external institutions and organizations that more traditional companies may ignore. New ideas that lead to innovation come from the synergies they experience when they interact with people from the government and non-governmental organizations (NGOs), as well as with academia, and with other businesses. For instance, Dow has had an external advisory council working with them on sustainability-related challenges since 1992. They suggest that the exposure to perspectives from the outside fuels their own innovation.[3]

All these cultural characteristics make sustainable companies more resilient than others. And resilience is a critical aspect of becoming change-adept. Let's take a closer look.

Resilience: a critical quality for handling change

To survive these days, when disruption is the norm rather than the exception, organizations and the people in them must be resilient. Let's start by looking at a classic example of a company that was not resilient when faced with disruption.

Case: Blockbuster – and the lack of reactive resilience

In the late 1990s, when mail-order video company Netflix was a startup, Blockbuster, the premiere retail video company, was doing very well with its bricks and mortar model. When the on-line video rental company Netflix came along, their founder proposed a partnership with Blockbuster. Blockbuster turned him down.[4]

Over the next few years, Blockbuster proved unable to change. Due to their flawed business model, they were locked in to maintaining the status quo. The predicament was that much of their profit came from late charges instead of rental fees. This weak spot in their business model became a pitfall for the company as they attempted to move into an on-line market. The company was not resilient enough to cope with the disruption in their market caused by Netflix. By the time they realized the danger, it was too late. Blockbuster filed for bankruptcy in 2010. And Netflix has gone on to achieve great success.[5]

Blockbuster lacked reactive resilience – or staying power. Reactive resilience includes the ability to absorb shock, cope, adjust, bounce back, and resume previous levels of performance in the face of unexpected threats. When challenged with changing conditions, companies with reactive resilience can adapt. They are agile. They are tough and can recover when facing adversity. This kind of staying power, which Blockbuster lacked, is a minimal requirement for long-term survival.[6]

Case: Starbucks and the power of transformative resilience

While Blockbuster illustrates a lack of basic adaptability and reactive resilience, the Starbucks story illustrates the power of transformative resilience, or the ability of companies to reinvent themselves when faced with threatening change. Starbucks was wildly successful before the financial crisis of 2008. However, the recession hit them hard. Over a period of two years, Starbucks closed hundreds of stores and saw a very large drop in profits. However, under the leadership of Howard Schultz, the company transformed its strategy from focusing on technology to "reigniting the emotional attachment to its customers." And they engaged their community of customers. The "My Starbucks Idea" campaign enabled customers to have a say in the company direction. Starbucks implemented many of these ideas and strengthened their relationship with customers at the same time. Their loyal customers continue to make them successful up to the present day. Starbucks has won many awards including "Best Business," "Most Admired Company," and "100 Best Corporate Citizens."[7]

Some companies, such as Starbucks, exceed the minimal requirements for surviving unexpected set-backs and demonstrate a type of proactive resilience often referred to as transformative resilience. When faced with unanticipated dilemmas, these companies focus on seizing opportunities rather than merely overcoming threats. Instead of simply coping, adapting, and bouncing back, they transform when faced with circumstances that could affect them negatively. They emerge stronger than ever before.[8]

Transformative resilience allows organizations to reinvent themselves through unique capabilities and cultures. Researchers have concluded that these resilient organizations possess a "blend of expertise, opportunism, creativity, and decisiveness despite uncertainty."[9] Sustainable companies possess all of these characteristics.

The transformative resilience of sustainable companies enables them to adapt and change continuously as they pursue their purpose. The nature of the challenges they tackle requires them to set a direction and stay the course, even though they may not know exactly where they will end up. Both reactive and proactive resilience are significant qualities for handling change well.

Enhancing change capacity

Our world challenges all of us to continuously increase our organizations' capacity for change. Some of you may already be leaders in sustainable organizations while others may want to move in that direction. Either way, the changes and disruptions that face us presently will continue to confront us in the future. And these challenges are becoming increasingly complex. Therefore, even if we believe that our companies are change-adept currently, we should not become complacent. Change will continue to push us to our limits. As leaders, we must continuously enhance our capacity for change by building change capabilities. First, we must build our own knowledge of change, which includes:

1   Understanding the dimensions of change.
2   Distinguishing among various types of change.
3   Challenging our own assumptions about change.

Change dimensions

Changes within organizations are inevitable and occur every day. However, the nature of these changes varies. Some are minor and require very little attention. Others are large-scale yet manageable with proper planning and execution. However, some changes are so complicated that leaders cannot map out an airtight strategy from the beginning. Most of us prefer changes that follow a predicable path that we can control. Certainly, small transitions that we can plan are easier to manage than large-scale or unplanned changes. However, in today's world, we are likely to face the need for all kinds of change, planned and unplanned, large and small.

Planned vs unplanned

In general, leaders like to know exactly where they are headed with a change so that they can manage it. With planned change, we can meticulously design a strategy for getting to concrete and measurable goals. Fortunately, most day-to-day changes fall into this category. For example, we can usually plan for the introduction and implementation of a new recycling program or the installation of a new piece of equipment. Even some large-scale changes, such as a move to a new facility, can be planned. While planned change can hit some bumps, we can still minimize the uncertainty. The leader's role is to develop, oversee, and monitor the implementation of the game plan and to address any unforeseen hiccups.

Unanticipated change can be very messy. Sometimes a crisis such as external activism or pressure from investors triggers the need for change that we didn't see coming. At other times circumstances such as shifts in customer preferences or the entrance of disruptive technologies into our markets catch us off-guard and force us to respond quickly. Unplanned change can create havoc. Therefore, it is in our best interest to minimize the need for it. Most likely, many surprises can be avoided if we are alert to the warning signs. Nonetheless, it is very likely that all of us will encounter some unforeseen situations that will call for change.

Small-scale vs large-scale

Some changes are so minor that they slip by us unnoticed. Others are large enough to overwhelm the best of us. We lack precise rules for differentiating a small change from a large one. However, usually we consider the number of people affected or how much the new state differs from the current one. For example, small-scale change might involve tweaks in a work process that is localized and quite manageable, or a slight adjustment in a policy that affects the entire organization. Large-scale change could include a move to a new facility or the overhaul of an organizational structure, for example.

We can still plan for some kinds of large-scale change. Strategic changes targeting concrete business objectives can serve as a good example of large-scale yet manageable change. For example, even though large-scale, we can still plan for the modification of products or services to meet the demands of customers or to address competitive threats. For instance, IBM's move from hardware to software and services is an example of strategic, large-scale change.

Determining whether a change is large or small isn't nearly as important as identifying who should participate in the process. Those who are most likely to be affected by a change should be included in the planning of it from the start. The larger the scale, the greater the need for widespread participation. Of course, high involvement works best with planned change and may not be feasible for crisis-driven change, no matter the scope, since crises require fast action. Very likely, decisions will rest with a few people who are in charge under crisis circumstances.

Types of change

While descriptions of change models and types abound, I will discuss three basic categories that I think have the most practical application. I have found the framework developed by change experts Ackerman and Anderson to be simple yet useful.[10]

Developmental

Change that merely improves what is already in place can be referred to as developmental change. Examples could include improving a skill or designing a more efficient way of carrying out a task. These small adjustments are sometimes referred to as continuous improvement or incremental change. Toyota, the multinational automobile manufacturer, has very successfully embedded developmental change into the culture. The word "kaizen" refers to continuous improvement or incremental change and is part of the Toyota philosophy and way of functioning.[11] Developmental change is finite – it has a beginning and an end. It can be managed from any part of an organization with or without senior leader involvement.

Transitional

Transitional change involves moving from what exists to something different yet clearly understood. For example, moving from one technology to another is transitional change. This kind of change is usually planned and quite controllable. The beginning and end states are both certain from the beginning. Therefore, the steps to move from one to the other are predictable. When the phrase "managing change" is used, it usually applies to a transitional change. As an example, one of our large global clients decided to outsource much of the IT operations in their company. This change had an impact on the entire organization in one way or another. And, of course, it truly affected all who worked within the company IT function. This initiative was a large-scale transitional change. The transition followed a clear path involving moving from one state to another. This change had a definite beginning and a clear end.

Transformational

Transformational change is radical. The future state is completely different from the present, therefore it involves more than how we do things. It entails a change in beliefs and values – or who we are. Transformational change is usually initiated by leaders at the top of an organization including the CEO. With transformational change those who lead it don't know the end state entirely as they start down the path. Leaders can set a direction and develop a high-level strategy for the change, but they cannot control it completely. These changes take many twists and turns and require constant monitoring and adjusting along the way. Traditional approaches to change management with tools for supporting it will not work with transformational change. In the words of Ron Ashkenas, writing in the *Harvard Business Review*:

> Transformation is another animal altogether. Unlike change management, it doesn't focus on a few discrete, well-defined shifts, but rather on a portfolio of initiatives, which are interdependent or intersecting. More importantly,

the overall goal of transformation is not just to execute a defined change – but to reinvent the organization and discover a new or revised business model based on a vision for the future. It's much more unpredictable, iterative, and experimental. It entails much higher risk. And even if successful change management leads to the execution of certain initiatives within the transformation portfolio, the overall transformation could still fail.[12]

Transformational change often requires fundamental shifts in the cultural foundations or identity of the organization since it challenges assumptions and values.

For example, companies that transform from a hierarchy where decisions are made top-down to a flatter structure with fewer managers and supervisors, will undergo transformation. Likewise, organizations that move from focusing on operational efficiency, uniformity, and chain of command to valuing collaboration, purpose, and shared vision will most likely face transformational change. While developmental and transitional changes don't require transformation, transformational change almost always includes developmental and transitional change as well. I discuss this topic in greater depth in Chapter 9.

Examining our assumptions about change

As I have worked with organizations over the years, I have encountered several assumptions about change that are unproven, at best, and in many cases just plain wrong. I refer to these beliefs as the change myths.

Assuming change will be simple

Change is more complex than many leaders envision. We all want change to be quick and painless. Yet change seldom goes exactly as planned and is rarely quick. Unless the change is small, very likely the process will experience some bumps. Stops and starts are common in any large-scale change process – especially if it is transformational.

Assuming that people are rational

Leaders who believe that they can merely announce a relatively large-scale change, explain the reasons for it, and move on are not being realistic. Even when people understand the purposes of change, those affected are likely to react emotionally. Yet many times leaders of change approach it from a purely rational angle. They seem to think that by offering the irrefutable evidence that change is necessary or should be desirable, people will willingly go along. This approach is unlikely to succeed. While individuals vary in their responses to change, emotions are almost always involved. Therefore, relying on only rational arguments will not get the job done.

Assuming resistance to change is inevitable

Emotional responses to change are not always signs of resistance. I do not believe that people always resist change. However, I do believe that change leads to ambivalence that often is interpreted as resistance. A person who expresses some doubts about a change is not necessarily a resistor. Almost all changes have pros and cons. And, generally, the larger-scale changes also bring ambiguity and uncertainty. Therefore, people may appear hesitant at first to embrace the changes wholeheartedly. Even those prompting and leading the change are likely to be ambivalent since, like everyone else, they face both the pros and the cons as well as the uncertainty.

Most of us are inclined to preserve stability and change usually threatens it. Since significant change disrupts the routines that help us cope with complexity, we are all likely to experience some distress. Nevertheless, discomfort doesn't always lead to resistance.

Assuming we can force change

Undoubtedly, many of us have fallen into the trap of thinking that we can change others through our power, sound arguments, strong relationships, or sheer will. However, take a minute to reflect, if you will, on whether you have ever truly been able to change others. Chances are, you, as I, would have to acknowledge a very modest track record. While we may be powerful enough to either coerce or inspire behavior change for the short term, no one can truly force maintainable change on anyone else. I am not implying that we have no effect on other people. However, while we certainly can influence others, we can't force lasting change. I discussed this topic in greater detail in Chapter 2.

As we give up these often-mistaken assumptions about change, we can find more effective ways to lead it. And the change process will be easier to lead if our organization is already good at making changes.

Personal challenges for leading change

To successfully guide our companies to becoming more change-adept, we must first attend to our own change-related capabilities. To take change in stride personally, we must tolerate uncertainty and ambiguity.

Becoming personally change-adept

Change can be challenging for any of us. When circumstances become unpredictable or ambiguous many of us may, at first, feel threatened and long to hold on to the familiar. Often such reactions only increase our anxiety and decrease the likelihood of effective responses. However, if we accept ambiguity as a fact of life and consciously raise our threshold for it, we are less likely to be anxious and more likely to make thoughtful decisions. While none of us controls our fate completely, by acting on those things that we can control we are likely to develop a greater sense of self-confidence which, in turn, leads to a greater sense of well-being. Many changes offer opportunities and threats. And oftentimes the threats that we fear are vague. Even concrete threats often fail to materialize.

How to increase our own tolerance for uncertainty and ambiguity

People differ in their tolerance for uncertainty and ambiguity. The more tolerant tend to handle change best. They tend to accept that some problems aren't solvable and recognize that life is ambiguous. When faced with change, they tend to consider their options, and avoid worrying about every detail. They tend to have confidence in their ability to handle whatever comes their way. Those with less tolerance for ambiguity tend to divide the world into "either/ or" categories and reject the idea that situations can be both positive and negative. They avoid making choices without complete information. They worry more in general and are more likely to resist change.[13]

The good news is that we can all increase our tolerance for uncertainty and ambiguity. A first step is to increase our self-awareness and identify the situations that tend to trigger our anxiety. Think about how you have reacted to past changes and identify patterns. As you approach change, attempt to nail down what you fear more specifically. When we can name our fears, we are in a better position to gain much needed perspective. As we begin to get a hold of our emotions we can assess the probabilities of what we fear happening. In many cases, we will find that the likelihood is low. Other times our fears may be quite realistic. In these cases, we can plan for how we will cope with the threats. When we recognize what we can take control of to some extent through our actions, we relieve some of our anxiety. As a leader, one of the most important things that you can do to create a change-adept organization is to increase your own tolerance for uncertainty and ambiguity.

Tips for coping with ambiguity and anxiety

The following are a few suggestions to consider (adapted with permission from "Tolerating Ambiguity" by Maggie Dugan[14]):

- **Stay neutral and suspend judgment**. Delay, if you can, the expression of an opinion, positive or negative, about the topic of discussion or exploration. Don't get distracted by the process either. Take it all in as interesting data.
- **Stay curious**. Seek to understand the things that would otherwise induce a judgment. Avoid assumptions, and try to take on an open-minded, curious stance about what's happening around you. Ask questions that start with "why" and say things like, "Tell me more about that."
- **Enjoy the mess**. The creative process is rarely neat and tidy. Consider change as an opportunity that allows you to be messy. The whole world is constantly demanding that you put things in order; give yourself permission to let them stay out of order, in service to a possibly more innovative outcome.

- **Take time**. The world that's asking for order is demanding speed as well. Slow things down and take your time to look at things longer, to ask more questions than you'd normally permit yourself, to generate more ideas and options before selecting among them.
- **Try things on**. Play with questions and ideas and concepts, try them on for size. Follow threads of thought, pretend something might work and see where it takes you. Live, temporarily, with possible options to see if they are useful or not.

Once you have become more change-adept personally, you will be in a better position to assist your organization in developing change capabilities. Assisting your organizations in embracing change, even in the face of uncertainty, may require you to take a different approach to framing change.

A fresh approach for leading change

Engaging in any kind of significant change is hard and very few organizations succeed in achieving their goals or initial vision. Leaders underestimate what it will take to succeed. Too often they delegate the change process to others as their own priorities shift. Many times, initiatives fall short because those leading the process failed to consider the people-side of change. These and many other pitfalls create legitimate concerns for all of us who wish to lead change. Perhaps it is time to take a new approach.

Overcoming deficit thinking

While I do not claim to have the answers for avoiding all the pitfalls, I do have years of experience in helping organizations with the people-side of change. Lack of employee engagement in the change efforts or downright resistance to the changes are among the most difficult challenges to address. Perhaps many of us are change-weary, partly because change initiatives often imply "deficit thinking." When we talk about change within this framework, people may believe that they have failed at what they have been doing, hence the change is necessary to make up for their deficits.[15] No wonder leaders cannot create excitement and engagement around change if it is couched in deficit thinking. I propose reframing change from how we can overcome our deficits to how we can build on our strengths to create something new and even better.

Inclusive change processes

When we talk about managing change, we may be implying that change will be done *to* people rather than carried out *with* people. I suggest that we talk about change as creating something new together. When change is inclusive, and people can apply their strengths and ingenuity to create it, change is more likely to engage rather than to repel. What better opportunity for employees to create meaning than to actively participate in bringing about new directions and growth for themselves and for their organizations – especially if the work involves contributing to the betterment of society.

To stimulate your thinking about new ways to frame change, I offer the following "what ifs" for your reflection as we move into the next section on deep change:

- What if we were able to create excitement in our organizations for the possibilities and opportunities that change can provide?
- What if we could ensure that people envision change as the occasion for personal and organizational growth?
- What if we positioned change as ways for people and organizations to better use their strengths?
- What if we approached change through collective conversations where people contribute to a shared vision that inspired everyone?

By shifting how we frame change and the processes through which we address it, we can increase our organizations' capacities for change.

Summary and conclusions

Sustainable companies have a better track record for change than others. They have developed the capabilities that enable resilience, both reactive and proactive. Their habit of challenging the status quo and emphasizing innovation enables them to predict and address events and possible disruptions that surprise others.

Change endeavors have dismal track records, in general. Those of us who wish to lead change in our own companies should understand the types and dimensions of change. By matching our change strategies to the nature of the change challenges, we can increase our effectiveness in leading it. If we are to be effective leaders of change we must start by increasing our own tolerance for uncertainty and ambiguity, and then build this capacity throughout our organizations. By changing our approaches from top-down initiatives grounded in deficit thinking to a more inclusive process that focuses on the future and builds on strengths, our efforts may be more successful.

Your turn: reflect on change

Now it is your turn to think about whether you personally and your company have the capabilities and systems to support change.

Assess your own change capabilities

Ask yourself how well you handle ambiguity. Read the questions in the column on the left and jot down your reflections and responses in the adjoining column on the right.

Reflection questions	Your thoughts
Do you feel threatened or energized when faced with ambiguous situations at work?	
What are the situations that are most likely to activate your anxiety and fear? And what do you tell yourself about these situations?	
How might you assess the probabilities of what you fear actually materializing?	
How might you reframe change from focusing on the threats to thinking about the opportunities? How might you talk to yourself in a different way as part of the reframing?	
What can you do to reduce your anxiety when you feel it coming on?	

Assess your organization

Reflection questions	Your thoughts
What is your company's track record with large-scale change? For example, a different business model, new physical location and/or building; change in products or services, new mission and/or vision?	
What is your company's track record in succeeding with small incremental change? For example, process improvements, adding new features to existing products or service, change in a policy.	

Think of a change that went well and one that did not go so well. In your opinion, what made a difference in the outcomes?	
How do you think people in your company deal with uncertainty? How could tolerance for uncertainty and ambiguity be improved?	
How has your company dealt with unwelcome surprises in the past?	
What practices are in place in your company to prevent or minimize these surprises?	
How does your company encourage and/ or enable people to reflect and learn?	

Notes

1 Robert Eccles, Kathleen Miller Perkins, and George Serafeim, "How to Become a Sustainable Company," *MIT Sloan Management Review* 53, no. 4 (Summer 2012): 43–50.
2 Eccles, Miller Perkins, and Serafeim, 2012, 49.
3 Kathleen Perkins, Robert Eccles, and Mark Weick, "Sustainability at Dow Chemical," *Journal of Applied Corporate Finance* 24, no. 2 (Spring 2012): 38–44.
4 Greg Sattel, "A Look Back at Why Blockbuster Really Failed and Why It Didn't Have To," *Forbes*, September 5, 2014. Available at: www.forbes.com/sites/gregsatell/2014/09/05/a-look-back-at-why-blockbuster-really-failed-and-why-it-didnt-have-to/#680dc5371d64.
5 John Antioco, "How I Did It: Blockbuster's Former CEO on Sparring with an Activist Shareholder," *Harvard Business Review*, April 2011. Available at: https://hbr.org/2011/04/how-i-did-it-blockbusters-former-ceo-on-sparring-with-an-activist-shareholder.
6 Kathy Perkins, "Are You Ready for the Surprises?" *Building Sustainable Legacies*, February 28, 2018, accessed September 8, 2018. Available at: https://building-sustainablelegacies.org/2018/02/28/are-you-ready-for-the-surprises.

7 Shezray Husain, Feroz Kahn, and Waqas Mirza, "Brewing Innovation," *Business Today*, September 28, 2014. Available at: www.businesstoday.in/magazine/lbs-case-study/how-starbucks-survived-the-financial-meltdown-of-2008/story/210059.html.

8 Ama Marston and Stephanie Marston, *Type R: Transformative Resilience for Thriving in a Turbulent World* (Public Affairs, January 9, 2018).

9 Cynthia A. Lengnick-Hall, Tammy Beck, and Mark Lengnick-Hall, "Developing a Capacity for Organizational Resilience through Strategic Human Resource Management," *Human Resource Management Review*, (2011), 21, 243–255.

10 Dean Anderson and Linda Ackerman Anderson, "What is Transformation, and Why is It so Hard to Manage?" Being First Inc., 2010, accessed September 8, 2018. Available at: http://changeleadersnetwork.com/free-resources/what-is-transformation-and-why-is-it-so-hard-to-manage.

11 Lean Manufacturing and Six Sigma Definitions website, accessed September 8, 2018. Available at: http://leansixsigmadefinition.com/glossary/kaizen.

12 Ron Ashkenas, "We Still Don't Know the Difference Between Change and Transformation," *Harvard Business Review*, January 15, 2015. Available at: https://hbr.org/2015/01/we-still-dont-know-the-difference-between-change-and-transformation.

13 Stanley Budner, "Intolerance of Ambiguity as a Personality Variable," *Journal of Personality*, (1962), 30, 29–50.

14 Maggie Dugan, "Tolerating Ambiguity," *Knowinnovation*, April 2, 2016. Available at: http://knowinnovation.com.

15 Kathy Miller Perkins, "Sustainability and Innovation: Creating Change That Engages the Workforce," *Journal of Corporate Citizenship*, (Summer 2012), 46, 175–187.

Part III

Deep change

The purpose of Part III is to explore how the patterns underlying our thinking affect how our organizations function and their ability to transform. Chapter 8 looks at mental models or the lens through which we view our experiences. This chapter differentiates the mental models of sustainable companies from others. It also examines how thinking biases affect our change capabilities. Chapter 9 draws from our research and the earlier chapters in the book to present a model for how to become a sustainable company. The chapter examines the transformational cycle and each stage in it. Subsequently the chapter explores transformational change in greater detail as well as what is required of leaders who undertake this kind of radical change.

Part III

Deep change

8 Mental models and change in sustainable companies

Chapter purpose

Do you ever wonder why our views of the world differ so widely yet all of us are certain that our own views are correct? And sometimes people, ourselves included, hold on to our views in the face of much contradictory evidence. Yet, as George Bernard Shaw once said, "Progress is impossible without change, and those who cannot change their minds cannot change anything."[1]

All of us make assumptions about ourselves, others, and how the world works. These frameworks are often referred to as mental models and they influence our judgments, attitudes, and behaviors. Those of us who have made major changes or transformations in our lives know that almost always we must change the way we think first. We must uncover and challenge our own assumptions, or the underlying beliefs that we take for granted, so that we can shift from old patterns of thinking to new.

Likewise, companies also hold mental models. And sustainable companies tend to hold different mental models than others. Their divergent ways of framing their role in the world lead to distinctive approaches to carrying out their business. They handle change better than others partly because of their unique mental models and awareness of how biases can influence their perceptions.

The purpose of this chapter is to examine the lens through which companies view how the world works. The chapter compares how sustainable companies differ from others in their views of their roles in society. The chapter will examine how these mental models relate to transformational change.

Mental models

Have you ever stopped to consider what is beneath how you think? We are thinking all the time, whether we want to or not. And my guess is that very seldom do we pause to muse about our own thinking. How often do you ask yourself whether you are thinking logically, accurately, thoroughly, or what you might be missing? We all rely on our own personal assumptions, which are often hidden. Your assumptions may differ from mine and we may not even know it. Our assumptions form frameworks that psychologists call mental models. They are beneficial because they help us rapidly organize information and make sense of our experiences. On the other hand, they can be detrimental if they inhibit our ability to change, as circumstances require it. Often an entire group, such as an organization, will share some of the same mental models. They come from a common history and shared experiences and they affect how we do business. They also have an impact on companies' flexibility and adaptability, and thus how we handle change.

What are mental models?

Have you ever wondered why you and a friend can view the very same situation yet reach different conclusions concerning what happened? And, often, both of you are confident that you are right and the other is wrong. Likewise, people with different political views can listen to the same evidence and yet argue over what it means.

These occurrences are very common and most likely stem from different assumptions or beliefs that we take for granted without proof. Our assumptions are the basis of our mental models, or underlying beliefs, about how the world works. These frameworks serve as filters for what we notice and how we interpret our experiences. They can be useful in preventing us from becoming overwhelmed. On the other hand, if the mental models become rigid, they can prevent us from changing even when circumstances require it.

Companies often hold collective mental models that help them make sense of the business world and how to navigate within it. However, as with individual mental models, when these assumptions become rigid and are never challenged, they can leave companies vulnerable to changes that may affect whether they survive, let alone succeed.

Individual mental models

To illustrate differing mental models, I offer the following examples. Some believe that everything happens for a reason. Others believe that many events tend to be random. Some think that human beings are naturally competitive while others believe that many prefer to collaborate. Many of us trust that we are in control of our own destinies, while others think that our outcomes are seriously affected by factors beyond our control. The list of different mental models is very long indeed. However, the important point is that we hold on to our mental models partly because we don't always know they exist and partly because they are useful for organizing our experiences. They allow us to simplify complex information. On the other hand, this simplicity limits how we view experiences. Oftentimes we can function more effectively when we understand the complexity of the challenges that face us.

Ideally, these frameworks change as we gain new knowledge and experiences. Unfortunately, mental models can be surprisingly stable. And while they can be useful, assumptions can get us into trouble. For instance, they can prevent us from getting along with others who think differently. They can certainly limit how much we are able to change and innovate.

Group mental models

Sometimes entire groups, such as companies, share mental models or ways of viewing the world. And group mental models can determine how our companies do business. In her book *Mental Models*, Kate Ward offers the examples of two insurance companies in the U.S.A. that operated with different mental models. Allstate assumed that customers would only be satisfied with personal service from local insurance agents. Progressive assumed that they could offer strong customer service on-line with lower costs.[2] These mental models led to two very different approaches to doing business.

Shared mental models can blind us to trends in the world that are likely to have an impact on our businesses. Thus, they can affect decisions critical to survival as well as to success. When people within a company hold common assumptions and remain resistant to other ways of thinking, they may miss trends that will either have a negative impact on them or prevent them from spotting positive opportunities.

Rigid and shared mental models can depress creativity and innovation. Often the most creative solutions come from people with different perspectives. When our mental models prevent us from seeing the value in new perspectives, our companies become vulnerable because we may miss opportunities. Steve Wozniak, cofounder of Apple Computers, tried and failed five times to convince Hewlett Packard that people would welcome personal computers. They rejected his suggestion that they manufacture them.[3] This is an astounding example of how the failure to challenge assumptions led to squandered fortunes.

Case: the utility crisis

A few years ago, we worked with a water and waste-water utility to help them address some much-needed changes. They had built their business on the assumption that they were the only game in town. After all, utilities have a monopoly, right? Wrong. They had been focused on some internal organizational issues that plagued them. And, as they would tell it later, they lost track of their customers' needs. Much to their surprise, one of their largest corporate customers built their own water facility, pulling revenue from the utility. Of course, this threw them into crisis. And their internal problems were magnified as a result. They failed to see a threat due to their shared, unquestioned, and inaccurate assumptions.

Mental models in sustainable companies

Companies operate with shared mental models that are fundamental to everything that goes on in the business. These frameworks influence how we view our company and its role in society. They influence our company identity, composed of purpose, vision, and values. Mental models have an impact on how we operate, who we view as our most significant stakeholders, and how we relate to them.

While the mental frameworks of sustainable companies vary in many ways from others, two related differences emerge as among the most critical: First, how they view the role of the corporation in society and, second, how they benefit from an outside-in vs inside-out approach to business. I consider these two frameworks to be the most significant because of their impact on how sustainable companies do business, how they relate to stakeholders, and how they approach change.

The role of the corporation in society

Consider the following two hypothetical examples of companies with very different assumptions about the role of the corporation in society:

- **Company A**: This company's culture is built on the assumption that business is largely separate from other aspects of society and exists to address the interests of their shareholders. Therefore, they define their company by the products and services they offer and the underlying capabilities that will enable them to maximize profits and create wealth for shareholders.
- **Company B**: This company's culture rests on the assumption that business is not distinct from the rest of society and that companies have a responsibility not only to stockholders but also to others both inside and out. Therefore, this company's identity speaks to larger societal issues. The leaders assume that they can achieve a balance between addressing the needs of their stockholders while also attending to the needs and expectations of other wide-ranging stakeholders such as customers, suppliers, activists, and communities.

I believe that ExxonMobil, a multinational oil and gas company, resembles Company A. As of August 2018, their website suggests that they aspire to be the best petroleum and petrochemical company in the world while following ethical principles. To achieve this vision, they focus on operations and finance.[4]

On the other hand, as an example of Company B, consider Dow, a multinational chemical corporation. They claim to be seeking breakthroughs for solving world challenges, while also becoming "the most profitable and respected science-driven chemical company in the world."[5]

The two companies differ in many ways, including their reputations for addressing climate change. In 2017 ExxonMobil was accused of communicating misleading information aimed at undermining public understanding of scientific knowledge about climate change. The accusation was that this behavior stemmed from favoring their own self-interest over evidence.[6] In reaction, the shareholders voted in favor of a climate change resolution against the advice of the Board of Directors.[7]

Dow has been acknowledged for the following:

- 17 times named to Dow Jones Sustainability World Index.[8]
- 11 U.S. Presidential Green Chemistry Awards – more than any other company.
- 2017 U.S. EPA Safer Choice Partner of the Year Award.[9]

Every company undoubtedly holds some collective mental models that are fundamental to how they function. The most socially responsible sustainable companies, more than others, tend to assume that they have a role to play in contributing to the well-being of society.

Outside-in vs inside-out thinking

Since socially responsible businesses view their role in society differently, it is not surprising that they also have distinct ways of approaching how they do business. Even though their businesses vary, they tend to think about their work similarly. They tend to rely on an outside-in rather than an inside-out framework for carrying out their missions. In their article, "Clarifying the Meaning of Sustainable Business,"[10] my colleagues Katrin Muff and Thomas Dyllick offer a framework for thinking about different approaches to business sustainability. They offer four simple categories.

> **Business as Usual – The Current Economic Paradigm**: The focus is on the economics of the business itself – e.g., cheap resources, efficient operations and creating value for shareholders. Since the companies begin with a focus on themselves, they refer to this as inside-out thinking.
>
> 1.0 **Refined Shareholder Value**: Recognition of environmental and social issues that raise threats and opportunities for businesses. They address these challenges within their existing business models and practices.
> 2.0 **Business Sustainability – Managing for the Triple Bottom Line**: The focus goes beyond shareholders and includes addressing the concerns of other stakeholders. They set sustainability-related goals aimed at reducing their negative impacts and measure and report progress while also focusing on how they can meet their goals economically and profitably. This too is inside-out thinking because the focus is still primarily on themselves and how they can do less harm to others.
> 3.0 **Business Sustainability 3.0 – Truly Sustainable Business**: These companies shift their focus from doing less harm to doing more good. They identify the societal challenges or needs that they might address and then assess how to use their capabilities and resources to do so. This is outside-in thinking.

This may seem confusing at first, so let's examine how these mental models function. Companies that take an inside-out approach start by assessing their capabilities and assets first when deciding what to produce. They may either focus solely on their own operations or include goals for how to do less harm to the environment and society. On the other hand, a company with an outside-in way of doing business starts by looking at the market place needs/societal problems first and then looks for ways to leverage their capabilities and assets to address problems. Often these companies also commit to innovation to address the issues that they confront. Consider the following examples of both mental models:

- Inside-out framework: Purpose is to make widgets or deliver a specific service based on current capabilities and assets. Emphasis is on offerings before needs.
- Outside-in framework: Purpose is to address a market/societal need. Emphasis is on needs before offerings.

From time to time my company has taken an inside-out approach but recently we have returned to the outside-in way of doing business. Our first step is to explore the problems that our corporate clients face. A few years ago, we found that corporations were suffering from organizational cultures that hindered their ability to achieve their sustainability goals. While knowing that we had capabilities to help companies with organizational culture change, we also knew that we did not have any culture assessment tools nor change processes targeting the exact nature of the need related to sustainability. Consequently, we decided to build on our existing capabilities and innovate. With the help of external partners, we developed a new assessment tool and acquired a platform for administering it. Our partners helped us with research that informed us on what to include in the assessment and then helped us validate the instrument. This is the work that ultimately inspired this book.

We still partner with others to analyze the assessment data so that we continuously increase our understanding of how the cultural pieces fit together to influence corporate sustainability. In addition to the assessment instrument, we developed a process for addressing the assessment results to help companies use the data to make necessary changes.

As you can see from my company's example, mental frameworks guide how companies function, including the promises of value that they offer to customers. As we shifted from an inside-out to an outside-in framework, we identified real issues impacting our clients' ability to pursue their purpose and benefit society. Then we looked at how we might use our capabilities to tackle the issues. We found that we did not have all the knowledge and skill that we needed to offer a complete solution to the problem. We addressed this quandary by forming partnerships with other persons and groups with the skills and knowledge to supplement our own capabilities. We now experience a valued and productive position in the marketplace while being true to our sense of mission.

Some companies start out with outside-in mental frameworks. Other companies have switched from inside-out to outside-in. Dow serves as a good example of a large company that made the switch. They used to describe themselves as a chemical company – an inside-out portrayal focused on what they produce. Now they describe themselves as a company that helps solve global problems – an outside-in characterization focused on societal needs. Likewise, Campbell Soups appears to be taking an outside-in approach. The Campbell Soups' website claims the company purpose is to provide "real food that matters for life's moments." They define real food as food that they would be proud to serve in their own homes. They are committed to a food philosophy that includes making food accessible to all, and producing food with recognizable ingredients based on plants and animals.[11]

This purpose-driven, outside-in approach is quickly becoming more mainstream. You will recall from Chapter 1, Blackrock CEO Larry Fink's statement that without a sense of purpose, no company can achieve its full potential. And that companies have a responsibility to provide benefit to all stakeholders while also succeeding financially.[12] Companies that are truly purpose-driven must approach their businesses with an outside-in mental framework. Purpose means contributing to the betterment of the world, not just producing widgets.

Mental models are beneficial in guiding us individually and helping us steer our companies. These frameworks provide us with a way to organize our experiences, our views of the world, and our place in it. However, our assumptions can get us into trouble when we fail to recognize them, or when they are rigid and unchanging. As human beings, we are subject to several thinking biases that serve to maintain our mental models even in the face of new experiences and contradictory evidence. I describe a few of the most prevalent and potentially damaging biases below.

Common thinking biases that prevent change

In his book *Thinking Fast and Slow*, Daniel Kahneman describes "a puzzling limitation of our mind: our excessive confidence in what we believe we know and our apparent inability to acknowledge the full extent of our ignorance and uncertainty of the world we live in."[13] I suspect that most of us consider ourselves to be logical thinkers. Yet, since we are human, we are all subject to thinking biases that can get in the way of logic. In fact, Kahneman describes approximately 20 biases that lead us to think less than rationally. When these biases are shared within a company they can be dangerous to the business because they lead to rigid, status-quo thinking, can lead to bad decisions, and prevent innovation. I will not cover all 20 of the biases. Rather, I have selected a few that I think are most important in our companies' decision-making and in our abilities to change.

Confirmation bias

Magicians who practice sleight of hand, or misdirection as they call it, count on our seeing what we expect rather than what is taking place in front of our eyes. And usually we do not let them down. We are all susceptible to seeing what we expect. Confirmation bias, or the tendency to seek out, notice, interpret, and remember information to protect our prior beliefs and expectations is widespread. It can and does affect how we treat each other within our organizations. For example, if I believe that a group of people is likely to resist a change that my company is considering, I am more likely to take notice of negative versus positive comments or behaviors related to the change. And I am likely to interpret the behaviors as resistance even though there may be other, more logical explanations such as valid concerns that I had not considered. When an entire organization falls subject to this bias, the leaders may miss important information that they need for developing sound strategies and making good decisions.

Curse of knowledge

The bias known as "the curse of knowledge" refers to our inability to communicate effectively when we are experts or have lots of information on a topic. We tend to summarize what we know and speak in abstractions that don't mean much to the less initiated. We may assume that the others share our knowledge, or we may be blind to the jargon and abstractions that we use. For example, most likely you share a common vocabulary with others in your group or department. Chances are that when you communicate outside of your group, some jargon creeps in that outsiders will not understand. Yet the words have become so commonplace to you that you don't realize that others outside of your group will have no idea what you mean. This bias can endanger our ability to collaborate across boundaries, or silos, within our own organizations, and is especially detrimental to our communicating and working with people outside of our companies.[14] Because we are unaware, we don't communicate with concrete examples and stories which work better than jargon and abstractions. This bias could explain why we aren't more effective at influencing others outside of our own group. The subcultures that spring up within departments and functions can hinder us from collaborating well with others if we make too many assumptions. A few years ago, I worked with a company that communicated through acronyms that others outside of the company did not understand. And, to make matters worse, different departments in the company used the same acronyms but assigned different meanings to them. You can imagine how confusing cross-departmental communication became.

False consensus, naïve realism

The "false consensus effect" refers to our tendency to overestimate the degree to which others agree with us. And the "naïve realism bias" is a tendency to believe that we see reality as it is and that others who disagree with us do not. When suffering from this bias, we view anyone who disagrees with us as irrational, uninformed, or overly subjective.[15] These two biases can create many problems within our cultures. Like the "curse of knowledge," these biases can prevent us from effectively collaborating with others. And if these biases permeate the entire organizational culture, our companies risk becoming so insular in their thinking that we miss the cues that are significant to our futures.

Assumptions can trip us up when we presume that everyone sees the world the way that we do. We may fail to benefit from the power of diverse thinking that fuels innovation and change. And most dangerous of all is the belief that those whose views of the world differ from our own are wrong. In truth, assumptions are merely our theories, hidden or not, of how things work. And theories aren't the same as truth.

Groupthink

Groupthink is a term used by social psychologists to describe group behaviors where everyone goes along with the dominant opinion of the group without examining diverse points of view. It occurs when cohesive groups hold tightly to shared assumptions and shut out any contradictory evidence. Even if some individuals in the group have doubts, they don't express them because they don't want to be impolite, don't like to confront, or are convinced that no one else has any qualms about the dominant opinion so they must be wrong. For whatever reason, even those with doubts choose to conform to what they believe to be the leading opinion. In defining groupthink, the dictionary states that it is characterized by self-deception and manufactured consent due to the need to conform.[16]

For example, in years past the American automobile industry made decisions based on the assumption that they were so superior in making cars that their automobiles would always remain the global favorites. Most likely due to some aspect of groupthink, they continued to operate with this assumption as the popularity of Asian and European cars rose. Likewise, during the early part of this decade, many of us acted as if home values would continue to rise indefinitely. Banks continued to issue bad loans and many of us borrowed against the equity we had built up in our homes. Of course, we all know what happened. Companies were ruined and many homeowners were hurt. When we ignore information that could contradict our assumptions so that we can hold on to our views, we put ourselves in peril.[17]

The most successful leaders think expansively. Thinking biases may dampen leadership effectiveness. Biases can prevent us from establishing the positive cultures that are in our own and our companies' best interests. Our rigid assumptions can keep us from building cultures that enable collaboration, innovation, and diversity. Biases can also prevent us from adapting mental models that may no longer match the world we work in, leaving us susceptible to obsolescence.

How to uncover our mental models and biases

We can't recognize the limitations of our mental models and biases if we don't know that they exist. Therefore, we must raise awareness of the possible flaws in our thinking. Uncovering our assumptions is not easy since we don't know what we can't see. However, we may be able to expose them by seeking out new experiences and information that could reveal other ways of viewing the world. Kate Ward suggests several tactics for revealing hidden assumptions.[18] For example, she recommends that we ask ourselves what we believe that others do not and then to reflect on the possible reasons for these differences. Likewise, we can attempt to separate observable facts from opinions – easier said than done. Nonetheless, the importance of our understanding the differences between the two cannot be overstated. Facts are observable and can be verified. Opinions are our interpretations and conclusions based on the facts. By separating opinions from facts, we can begin to uncover our own assumptions. We can learn more about assumptions by questioning others who have reached different conclusions from our own based on the same facts.

I attempt to challenge my own assumptions by intentionally looking for information that contradicts them. When I collect data of any kind as part of my research, I begin by asking myself whether my research methods would allow for my initial hunches to be disproven. Once I gather the data, I look for surprises – any information that seems to be incongruent with my theories. I contend that each of us should follow a similar process as we reflect on our own experiences.

Within our organizations, we must be willing to examine and challenge the assumptions that underlie our mental models. None of us wants to face unpleasant surprises due to our reliance on inaccurate and outdated assumptions. As we continuously challenge the status quo, we prevent rigidity in our thinking.

Tips for challenging the status quo

Because of the speed of change, our companies must be agile and resilient. That means we should always encourage everyone in the company to examine their own mental models by challenging the status quo. Consider doing the following:

- Normalize the examination of varying points of view before making decisions. For example, you might require decision-makers to consider strategies contrary to the most readily acceptable before landing on a path forward.
- Create an environment where disagreement is not only viewed as desirable but necessary. Perhaps you can appoint naysayers to consciously take the opposite point of view from the majority to make productive disagreeing normative.
- Encourage true diversity – not just the kind you can see but diversity in how people think. Instead of recruiting and hiring only people who will fit into your culture readily, look for the disruptors. Remember the story of Steve Woznick, the inventor of the personal computer? He pitched his invention to his employer Hewlett Packard five times before giving up and forming the Apple computer company with Steve Jobs.

- Test assumptions. Create the expectation that all will lay out their assumptions when offering opinions. This will be difficult at first, because we are so often unaware of our assumptions. Nevertheless, people will improve over time and will learn to describe the assumptions that underlie their opinions.
- Look for stereotypes that are operating within your culture. For example, do most people assume that all millennials think differently than all baby boomers? Examine these stereotypes carefully and avoid noticing only what you believe to be true initially – the confirmation bias.

Summary and conclusions

All of us view the world through our own mental models. We take these frameworks for granted, and often assume that our own world view is the only correct one. We are also susceptible to thinking biases that can inhibit our effectiveness in working with others and making rational decisions. Often groups that share a common history, such as companies or departments within them, also share a collective mental model and fall victim to the same biases. If we are to become agile and resilient, we must challenge our own individual and collective frameworks and biases. If we are to become change-adept, both personally and as organizations, we must learn how to uncover and challenge the assumptions that underlie our thinking and our functioning.

Your turn: assessing how we think

The greater our awareness of how we think, both individually and as a company, the more agile, innovative, and effective we can become. The following reflections are aimed at raising our awareness.

Part 1: uncovering our thinking biases

Reflect on the last time you had a conflict or disagreement with someone at work that didn't end well. Describe how you handled it. Then review your description looking for possible biases and assumptions that influenced your response. If you should encounter a similar conflict in the future, how might you check on the accuracy of your assumptions?

Description of the conflict and how you handled it	What worked and what failed? Do you spot any biases? Describe these	What could you do differently next time you are in a similar situation?

Reflect on the last time you attempted to persuade someone to consider your point of view. Were you successful? Why or why not? If not, do you think that any biases affected the outcomes?

Description of the situation	*Reflection on why you succeeded or failed to persuade*

Part 2: inside-out or outside-in

Is your company's mental model inside-out or outside-in? What about your own department or other area of influence? As you reflect, jot down your thoughts below. Include some descriptions of how you reached your conclusions. What do you see, hear, experience that leads you to attribute this mental framework to your company? To your department?

My company:	**My department/area of influence:**

If your department or other area of influence does have an inside-out approach, what can you do to change it to outside-in? What would be different if you made this switch?

Steps I can take:	**What would be different:**

Your turn: act to address mental models

Jot down some actions that you will take to examine your own personal mental models. Then list some actions you might take to look at the mental models operating in your department, function, or part of the company.

Actions I will take on my own:
Actions I will take in my area of influence:

Notes

1 George Bernard Shaw quotes. *BrainyQuote.com*, BrainyMedia Inc., 2018, accessed October 29, 2018. Available at: www.brainyquote.com/quotes/george_bernard_shaw_386923.

2 Kate Ward, *Mental Models* (King of Prussia, HRDQ, 2012), 17.

3 Julie Bord, "Hewlett Packard Could Have Been Apple if Not for 5 Bad Decisions," *Business Insider*, February 1, 2013. Available at: www.businessinsider.com/woz-begged-hp-to-make-the-apple-pc-2013-2.

4 "Our Guiding Principles," ExxonMobil Corporation website accessed August 29, 2018. Available at: https://corporate.exxonmobil.com/en/company/about-us/guiding-principles.

5 Robert Eccles, George Serafeim, and S Xin Lee, "Dow Chemical: Innovating for Sustainability," *Harvard Business School Case N9-112-064* (January 25, 2012).

6 Geoffrey Supran and Naomi Oreskes, "Assessing ExxonMobil's Climate Change Communications (1977–2014)," *Environmental Research Letters* 12, no. 8, August 23, 2017. Available at: http://iopscience.iop.org/article/10.1088/1748-9326/aa815f/meta.

7 Megan Darby, "Exxon Shareholders Win 'Historic' Climate Vote Against Board's Advice," *Climate Home News*, May 31, 2017. Available at: www.climatechangenews.com/2017/05/31/exxon-shareholders-win-historic-vote-climate-transparency.

8 "DowDupont Named to Dow Jones World Sustainability Index," Dow Corporate website accessed August 29, 2018. Available at: www.dow.com/en-us/news/press-releases/dowdupont-named-to-dow-jones-sustainability-world-index.

9 "Dow Science and Sustainability Highlights and Reporting," Dow Corporate website accessed August 29, 2018. Available at: www.dow.com/en-us/science-and-sustainability/highlights-and-reporting.

10 Thomas Dyllick and Katrin Muff, "Clarifying the Meaning of Sustainable Business: Introducing a Typology from Business as Usual to True Sustainability," *Organization and Environment*, (2016), 29, no. 2, 156–174.

11 Campbell Soup Company website, accessed on August 29, 2018. Available at: www.campbellsoupcompany.com/about-campbell.

12 Larry Fink's Annual Letter to CEOs: "A Sense of Purpose," Blackrock website accessed September 8, 2018. Available at: www.blackrock.com/corporate/investor-relations/larry-fink-ceo-letter.

13 Daniel Kahneman, *Thinking Fast and Slow* (New York: Farrar, Straus, and Giroux; 1st edition, October 2011).

14 Ship Heath and Dan Heath, "The Curse of Knowledge," *Harvard Business Review*, December 2006. Available at: https://hbr.org/2006/12/the-curse-of-knowledge.

15 "List of Cognitive Biases," *Wikipedia*, 2018. Available at: https://en.wikipedia.org/wiki/List_of_cognitive_biases.

16 "Groupthink," definition, *Merriam-Webster Dictionary*, accessed on September 19, 2018. Available at: www.merriam-webster.com/dictionary/groupthink.

17 Jason DeMers, "How Groupthink Can Cost Your Business," *Entrepreneur*, April 16, 2018. Available at: www.entrepreneur.com/article/311864.

18 Ward, 2012, 22.

9 The Transformational Cycle

Becoming a sustainable company

Chapter purpose

Organizational transformation is profound. While it begins with a vision, often based on imagination, vision alone is not enough. The process of transforming requires hard work, persistence, and vigilance, sometimes over years. It is dramatic and emotional, invigorating and frightening. Transformation has an impact on people personally as it challenges long-held beliefs and values. A company can change without transforming but cannot transform without changing. Companies can certainly become *more* sustainable through incremental changes and without taking on radical transformation. However, to become truly sustainable in the way I have defined it in this book, many companies will choose to transform.

The purpose of this chapter is to look at the predictable cycle that characterizes companies not merely changing but transforming to become truly sustainable. I present a model of the Transformational Cycle followed by an exploration of transformation at a deeper level, including what it requires of leaders.

How to become a sustainable company: Transformational Cycle

You will recall that my colleagues and I began our work on sustainable cultures by asking two questions:

1   What do sustainable companies do that others do not? The previous chapters addressed this question.
2   How do sustainable companies change to support implementation of broad-scale sustainable strategies? I will address this question in this chapter.

In our 2012 research and subsequent article,[1] my colleagues and I described a path to becoming a sustainable company to answer this second question. Our answers assumed that to become truly sustainable, a company had to reframe its identity and thus transform. However, over the subsequent years of my research and practice, I have concluded that companies can become *more* sustainable through less dramatic changes than our original model implied. However, to become *truly* sustainable, most companies will indeed need to transform, that is, to change who they are and what they believe in addition to modifying how they function.

The following illustration, The Transformational Cycle, is based on my research concerning how companies transform to become truly sustainable.

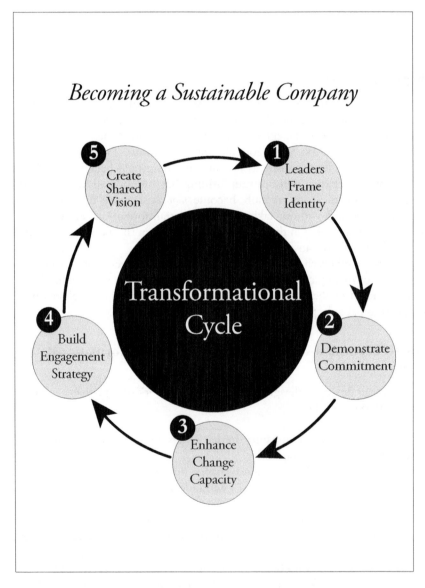

Figure 4 Becoming a sustainable company

Stages to becoming a sustainable company

The cycle is composed of five predictable stages that represent ongoing processes that may continue to evolve over years. Sometimes the stages overlap and what happens in one stage almost always reinforces the next. Stage 1 entails framing or reframing the company identity, usually by the CEO. The reframing is followed by Stage 2 in which leaders demonstrate their commitment to the new identity by embedding it into the strategies and operations of the company. In Stage 3 the focus is on enhancing the organization's capacity for change both through building a supportive internal culture and establishing new kinds of relationships with people and organizations outside of the company's boundaries. Stage 4 follows closely on the heels of the previous stage and involves developing and implementing an engagement strategy which leads to Stage 5. In this stage the vision that came from the reframing of the identity is built out across the organization so that ultimately it is shared across the entire organization and incorporated into everyone's work. As the vision comes alive in every corner of the company, it leads to greater understanding of the identity which infuses it with more depth. Thus, the cycle repeats and continues. Now that I have provided this overview of the cycle, let's take a closer look at each stage.

Stage 1: frame the company's identity

First, leaders frame or reframe the company identity as a sustainable enterprise. As a result of our many studies over the years, we have concluded that this act requires a strong commitment from the top-level leadership, which sometimes comes from pressures inside the organization but more often originates from leaders' connections with groups outside the organization's boundaries. In either case, the pressures, interactions, and exposures to different ways of thinking lead to a shift in the leaders' mental models, specifically their perceptions of the role of the corporation in society. Through their own personal commitments to becoming sustainable, they create a vision for the company that is clear and inspiring. The most successful leaders support their vision with a strong business case. Employees begin to understand the vision and its importance to the company as a result.

Stage 2: demonstrate commitment

While employees may understand the new vision when leaders are clear and inspiring, they will believe in its importance only when they see behaviors and systems that support it. Therefore, in this second stage, leaders begin to build trust by demonstrating a strong personal commitment to the vision. Our research shows that leaders establish their commitment by adopting a longer-term view of the business and incorporating the new identity, values, and commitments into their decision-making. In addition, they show that they are willing to take measured risks in pursuit of their vision and goals. They enable people to learn continuously and they encourage employees to gain knowledge from people outside of the company. When employees observe their leaders' actions, they begin to trust them and accept the vision.

Stage 3: enhance change capacity

A purpose-driven identity that integrates social and business impact requires a different kind of internal culture and new relationships with externals. Therefore, unless a company is "born sustainable," meaning created with a mission balanced between purpose and profits, many aspects of the company culture will need to change.

As I discussed in Chapter 4, trust is the anchor for change. Ideally, trust will be strong already, even before the company attempts to change. However, transformation requires very high levels of trust. While sustainable companies do have a stronger track record for both large-scale and small incremental change, leaders should not be complacent. Successful change hinges on widespread trust that must be nurtured. The changes required by a new identity are often made in an atmosphere of uncertainty; therefore, trust becomes more critical than ever and it is fragile. Fostering trust is one of the main responsibilities of leaders in this stage. In our 2012 article we concluded:

> Trust grows when people perceive that they are part of a collective effort to deliver value to stakeholders in a way that contributes to the betterment of their world. Work becomes more meaningful, and people become more engaged and productive.[2]

Stage 4: build engagement strategy

Employee engagement is a byproduct of meaningful work where employees believe that they make a difference.[3] Therefore, employees begin to truly buy in to the vision when they understand how their own work connects with it. Leaders of sustainable companies usually have a clear strategy for engaging employees in the vision.

Stage 5: create shared vision

As all employees begin to understand and accept the vision, they begin to define it as it applies to them in their own jobs. This is how a shared vision emerges. Employees develop a keen understanding of how they contribute to carrying out the company purpose and pursuing the vision. Work becomes more meaningful to them and they engage. Their engagement is especially strong if they believe that their contribution is recognized and valued by others, especially by people in formal leadership roles.

They strengthen their belief in the importance of sustainability to the company's long-term success. At this point, employees are acutely aware of their company's values and they care about its reputation with the public. One of the strongest patterns in our data is this: When people buy into a shared vision and believe that a commitment to sustainability is critical to the company's business success, their level of engagement with their work and with the company increases. The greater their belief in the importance of sustainability to the company, the more engaged they become.

The next section will build on the Transformational Cycle and examine the nature of transformational change in greater depth.

Transformational change overview

Organizational transformation is a radical change that touches every part of the company and requires great persistence. Therefore, leaders should not undertake a transformational process without reflecting on whether they have the courage and tenacity to see it through. The process is hard and can take years to accomplish. It requires a clear vision and great tolerance for uncertainty and ambiguity. Because the path is almost never clear in the beginning, transformation requires taking risks and engaging in trial and error. Many companies try to transform and fail due to shifting priorities or underestimating either the effort required or the obstacles to overcome. Nevertheless, some companies do succeed in transforming.

Often companies begin a transformational change process when a leader breaks with the historical views of company identity. At times leaders gradually reach the point of desiring transformation by undertaking several other types of change first. In either case, once leaders commit to transformation, they initiate a change in company identity. They do this by establishing a direction and developing a vision. However, they cannot control the transformational process entirely. It unfolds through social interactions across the organization ultimately leading to a shared vision.

While the CEO invariably initiates the transformation and holds the ownership of it for a while, he or she almost always secures the assistance of others such as internal high-level leaders and/or external consultants referred to as change agents. Nevertheless, the CEO retains sponsorship of the transformation while the internal and external change agents may oversee the development and implementation of a portfolio of change initiatives and strategies that will evolve over time. The change agents also assist with the customization of the plans to the local needs throughout the company as the entire organization begins to transform.[4]

Strategic vs transformational change

Transformational and strategic change do share some commonalities. They are both large in scale and likely to impact a broad swath of an organization. And each may require some modifications in how the company is structured and how work is organized. Nevertheless, strategic and transformational changes aren't exactly alike. While transformation almost always includes strategic change, strategic change does not always lead to transformation.

Strategic change most often results from some outside pressure such as new customer demands or disruptive technologies. Sometimes it is triggered by the recognition of opportunities such as new markets or the creation of different products. On the other hand, transformational change is set in motion when the leader of the company begins to question its foundational beliefs, assumptions, and values. As I mentioned previously, this questioning can be promoted by a crisis instigated from external activism or the introduction of a new CEO with a fresh perspective. Other times, the transformation comes about when leaders are exposed to new ways of thinking, usually from outside the boundaries of their own organizations. Of course, the transformation could result from a combination of factors.

Case: Interface – a story for change

The case of Interface, the world's largest modular carpeting manufacturer described in previous chapters, illustrates a transformation that came about when a leader was exposed to different thinking. As you will recall, Interface began to transform when the CEO, Ray Anderson, shifted how he viewed the company's role in society. Ray Anderson was an entrepreneur who founded the company and ran it based on common and traditional values focused on profits. The modular carpets were heavily reliant on fossil fuels. In 1994, Anderson was asked to present his company's environmental policies. The request caught him by surprise since he later admitted that he did not have any such policies. About the same time, he stumbled across Paul Hawkins' book, *The Ecology of Commerce.*[5] Anderson claimed to have had an epiphany. He concluded that his company was "plundering the earth" and had to change course. This story has now become legend. As the company's underlying beliefs about its role in society shifted, they made a firm commitment to do less harm. Consequently, the company foundations now include strong values related to environmental respect and stewardship. While Interface began this journey by focusing on doing less harm, over time they also committed to doing more good.[6] Their vision now focuses on revolutionizing the industry. And the company still honors the values that Anderson instilled.

Case: PepsiCo, Performance with Purpose

Food and Beverage Company PepsiCo serves as an example of how transformation of a company started with a new leader. PepsiCo's change began shortly after Indra Nooyi became the CEO. Her vision was to create a company of character and she pushed to take on the challenge of the growing obesity epidemic in society. She integrated her vision with a business case based on the belief that this trend would ultimately lead to a demand for healthier foods. In 2007, PepsiCo launched Performance with Purpose. Recently she stated, "From day one, Performance with Purpose has been about the way we make money, not the way we spend it. It is about the character of our company."[7] In 2010 PepsiCo announced the goal of building a $30 billion nutrition business by the year 2020. They expanded their research and development team to include world-renowned medical doctors, nutritionists, and food scientists who worked together to develop new products. They were aiming for breakthrough innovation in the creation of healthy snacks.

Some have argued that PepsiCo's transformation took place in only part of the company. They did not abandon their popular sugary snacks altogether. Nevertheless, they did reduce the sugar and salt content of many. And their healthy snacks (which they refer to as guilt-free snacks) business is growing. It currently accounts for 45 percent of their revenue. So, is Performance with Purpose a partial or complete company transformation? Hard to say. Transformation is complex, evolves over a long time period, and is never over.

Transformation as deep change

Transformational change is often uncomfortable, especially for leaders who face the need to relinquish some of their power and control. Robert E. Quinn, chair of the Department of Organizational Behavior and Human Resource Management at the University of Michigan School of Business, entitled his book on transformational change *Building the Bridge as You Walk on It*.[8] He suggests that leaders must move towards what he calls "deep change." This involves becoming purpose-centered and putting the welfare of others before our own selfish needs. It also entails opening to new experiences. To enter this unknown territory, we must be willing to be vulnerable.

In his writing about transformational change, Robert Gass, psychologist, organizational consultant and musician, suggests that it requires us to change our problem-centered mental models to focus on a positive vision. While he acknowledges the importance of critical thinking, he asserts that we must also honor what is good, useful, and possible. Those of us with a control mindset must learn to balance it with letting go. He suggests that we look at transformation as a dance rather than an attempt to dominate life. Sometimes we need to let the change emerge instead of forcing it.[9] To do so, many of us will need to shift our own mental models of what it means to lead.

When we think of change, most likely we are envisioning transitional change that follows a predictable and rational process that we can manage and control. However, transformational change does not work like transitional change. Transformation deals equally with the hearts and minds of people and involves breakthroughs in beliefs and behaviors, argues Gass. We cannot put together a tight and unbending budget for transformation nor outline every step and time-line on a project plan. It is not an initiative to be "rolled out" – a phrase commonly used to describe the launching of a new strategy or plan. The familiar tenets of change management and the tools that support it are unlikely to work perfectly with transformation.

I do not mean to imply that leadership and strategies are unimportant nor that the process is completely unmanageable. As Bryan de Lottinville, CEO of Benevity, said about his own organization, "Culture is made up of a thousand little things." And each of these thousand little things may require conscious planning for alignment with the purpose and vision. Thus, once the vision and direction are clear and shared, the implications for the culture and the systems that support it may be addressed more systematically. Nevertheless, the overall reinvention of the organization is a fluid process.

Companies that seek transformational change quite often fail to achieve it. Global consultancy Bain and Company reports that only 12 percent of corporate transformation programs succeed in reaching or exceeding the goals. Furthermore, only 2 percent achieve their goals when the transformation is focused on sustainability.[10] This low level of success may be attributed to many factors including resistant cultures, shifting priorities, and lack of a vision that inspires and engages employees. However, it may also be a result of our relying on the wrong mental models and failing to relinquish any control. Let's take a look at an example of a company that succeeded in transforming by redistributing control.

Case: building trust – transforming the culture

One of our clients, the Chemical Company, illustrates what an organization can achieve when it transforms its culture with the goal of rebuilding trust. This transformation resulted from a crisis. The Chemical Company had two strong labor unions that often clashed with management. Over the years the relationship became increasingly adversarial until eventually the conflict resulted in a brutal strike which included some violence. As in most of these cases, a strike was in no one's best interest. Management and labor alike recognized the futility of their mistrust and animosity. They decided to take the risk of transforming their organization. They were looking for a new way to work.

The top-level leader had a vision of a company committed to trust, collaboration, and the redistribution of power. He believed that the company existed to produce great products and to provide strong returns to shareholders. However, and equally important, he believed that the company existed to create a new kind of workplace where people at all levels were empowered to make decisions, grow, and use their knowledge and skills to contribute to a collaborative community that ran the business. He wanted to establish a company based on respect and dignity for all and committed to the worth of every person in it.

The president of the company held a meeting with the entire organization to set the tone for the transformation. He committed to transparency and began to share business data freely with everyone in the company. He committed to involve all in the transformation. This was not going to be a top-down effort. The senior leaders pledged to work with everyone to establish a variety of mechanisms for employee involvement. People from all levels of the company were instrumental in putting together a plan for a transformed culture. Work groups met to create processes for distributed versus centralized decision-making that pushed control from the top out to the entire organization.

The transformation required everyone to work differently and, therefore, people needed new skills and knowledge. All employees received training that included focusing on proficiencies in areas such as group processes and meeting preparation. Other training included knowledge for decision-making and capabilities for collaboration. As a result, employees were well prepared to play their part in the new organization.

Together employees from all levels established a plant-wide, cross-level, and cross-functional steering committee to work towards culture change with emphasis on how the various groups throughout the organization would relate to each other and work together. This group addressed issues that came up, set standards and protocols, and supported the training and development of everyone on both technical and interpersonal skills.

Power that had been held at the top of a hierarchy was redistributed as layers of supervision were eliminated. All employees gained increased control over their own work. As a result, they understood more clearly how they contributed to company success and community well-being.

The top-level leadership actively participated in the cross-level and cross-functional teams. People took on tasks based on their expertise and levels of knowledge rather than their positions. As trust grew, people became increasingly willing to take risks to enable the company and the people in it to thrive. The outcomes of these innovations included a decline in worker grievances and turnover, an improvement in the safety record of the plant, as well as an increase in productivity. Customer complaints dropped, and costs of production went down.

While this transformation was exciting, trust was not rebuilt overnight; it was developed through sustained hard work and some risk-taking. Over time, people began to give each other the benefit of the doubt and engage in collective conversations to hear and understand the perspectives, needs, and issues of the others. Rather than protecting turf and digging in when disagreements arose, all committed to collaborate to solve problems.

This company transformed to pursue a purpose centered on facilitating the growth, development, and well-being of everyone employed by the company. Their commitment was to balance this purpose with profits. And they succeeded. They became the model for other companies that wanted to create this type of workplace.

Developing the capacity for transformational change

The mindsets and mental models that enable transformational change are unlikely to be in the repertoires of more traditional leaders. If we are to succeed in leading transformational change in our organizations, we must first look at ourselves and our own capacities for change. We must be willing to entertain new ways of looking at the world and functioning in our roles.

Developing the personal capacity for transformational change

Have you ever wondered why you feel so open to change yet believe that others resist it? Undoubtedly many of us assume that the barriers to change lie elsewhere – certainly not within ourselves. Yet my experience in working with change is that we are often blind to our own defenses against it. And as leaders, we must examine our personal capacities to transform ourselves if we wish to lead successful transformations in our organizations.

What readiness for change really means

Most of the time leaders in our client organizations tell me that they are certainly ready for an organizational culture change. However, I have learned that their definitions of "readiness" may fall short of what change will require. For example, some believe that they are ready merely because others have told them that change is needed in the organization. More often, when they say that they are ready, they mean that they are ready for others to change. They fail to consider that they may need to change themselves. Sometimes they truly mean that they are ready to do whatever it takes personally to ensure that the organization can follow a path to successful change. Even when they sincerely commit to personal change, their own assumptions about this undertaking may miss the depth and complexity of what they are taking on.

If you truly desire to lead change, especially if you want to engage your organization in a transformation, I challenge you to consider whether you are ready to reflect on your assumptions and bring your own blind spots to light. You will be ready to lead transformational change in your organization only after you have examined your personal capacities for transformation.

Stages of readiness for change

Personal readiness for change is not an either/or proposition – i.e., either you are ready or you are not. Readiness occurs in stages.[11] The first stage is to become aware that we need to change. Leaders at the top of their organizations often view themselves as infallible. They believe that they have risen to their level of authority because of their own impeccable knowledge, skill, and perhaps personality. Since what they have done in the past has worked for them, they don't question the path that they are on. This is one of the highest hurdles to overcome. When you are engaged with changing the identity of the organization, the skills that have worked for you in the past are unlikely to suffice.

Once we recognize the need for personal change, we can begin to contemplate what it means for us. However, we may still be ambivalent and therefore not yet prepared to act. Leaders can get stuck in this stage. Even if you are aware of your own personal limitations and how your behaviors may block change, you may still lack the motivation to act. Leaders often fail to progress beyond this stage due to their own ambivalence, intolerance for uncertainty, anxiety, or shifting priorities. However, those who persevere move to the third stage of change. They come to terms with their shortcomings and start planning for their own transformation.

If you truly want to transform yourself in preparation for leading the transformation of the organization, begin by focusing on how you think, including examining your own mental models and mindsets.

Change and action logics

Over the last decade a group of professors and practitioners have developed an approach to transformational leadership that focuses on the development of action logics, which they define as how we interpret our surroundings and how we act when our power is threatened.[12] According to their research, most of us are conventional thinkers. We are very likely to either rely on our own knowledge and expertise to guide our behavior or to focus on our specific goals, objectives, and deliverables. We may not reflect much on our underlying assumptions nor question whether our expertise will enable us to be most effective. We almost certainly do not question the validity of our goals or our process for developing strategies. While these conventional action logics may serve us well in some circumstances, transformation is very likely to require different ways of thinking about our organizations and the challenges we face.

The body of research on action logics has shown that successful transformational leaders think differently. While they are interacting with others, they are aware of their own thought processes and feelings as well as their own limitations. And they realize that others may be framing situations differently.[13] They are willing to give up control and to become vulnerable. They lay out their own assumptions for others to challenge. They are highly collaborative and open to other points of view. In fact, they intentionally seek to understand mental models different from their own. They tend to handle conflict well and are good at developing shared visions.

I have barely skimmed the surface of action logics in my description of it. Any of you who truly wish to engage in organizational transformation should delve more deeply into this work and reflect on its implications for your own capacity for change.

Transforming ourselves through action

Upon accepting the need to change, leaders must do what it takes to develop their capacities to transform themselves and their organizations simultaneously. If you reach this stage, most likely you will begin to act differently, and others will take notice. You become a model for what you hope to achieve throughout the organization. However, you also realize the complexity of change. You understand that there are no simple solutions. Nevertheless, with a strong commitment to the transformation and a desire to collaborate with others, you can find ways to develop personally and remove the barriers to organizational transformation. While these personal challenges are not easy to address, if we truly want to lead change, we must look at ourselves first.

Developing the organizational capacity for transformational change

As we prepare our organizations for transformation, we are in uncharted territory due to the complexity of this type of radical change. Instead of carrying out one or two initiatives, transformation involves engaging in an entire portfolio of changes. As a top-level leader you will set the direction for the transformation. However, you are unlikely to have a clear path in mind nor even a firm end-point. Remember, you will be building the bridge as you walk on it.[14] You will need to enroll everyone throughout the company in the process of clarifying what the vision means in their own jobs and defining the paths for moving towards it.

Action inquiry, action research, and action learning provide fresh methods for bringing people together to achieve transformational change. While there are several variations within these approaches, the basis of all of them involves groups of people with diverse perspectives collaborating to tackle problems and opportunities while learning together. While I am not an expert on action learning, I believe that this approach, or one of the variations, holds the most promise of any of the change methodologies for bringing about transformations.

What is Action Learning?

The World Institute for Action Learning defines it as follows:

> Action Learning is a process that involves a small group working on real problems, taking action, and learning as individuals, as a team, and as an organization. It helps organizations develop creative, flexible and successful strategies to pressing problems.[15]

The promise of action learning lies in its effectiveness in dealing with complex problems where the goals are imprecise and the solutions aren't obvious. It is participatory rather than a top-down process, based on the premise that we need to seek new ways to solve problems rather than merely relying on the same methods that created the problems in the first place. The process involves small teams of people with diverse backgrounds and experience of collaborating. The team adopts an experimental mindset and begins with questions and reflections which serve to clarify the nature of the problem and possible solutions to it. Through the collective knowledge and synergies within the team, fresh solutions are likely to emerge. The team tries out the solutions and the members learn together as they reflect on the outcomes.[16] According to Christopher Juniper, Board President of the Action Research for Sustainable Enterprise in Collaborative Communities Network, "Organizational transformations occur incrementally, like an amoeba moving towards a new location, one small 'foot forward' at a time."[17]

While action learning can build an organization's capacity for transformation, practitioners stress that the approach succeeds only when individuals are open to personal transformation through the process as well. According to Bill Torbert, former Director of the Organizational Transformation Doctoral Program at Carroll Graduate School of Management at Boston College, "Action inquiry is a lifelong process of transformational learning that individuals, teams, and whole organizations can undertake if they wish to become increasingly capable of performing in effective, transformational, and sustainable ways."[18]

Summary and conclusions

Companies that transform to become sustainable follow a predictable cycle. It starts with the top-level leader reframing the company identity, followed by demonstrating a commitment to it by embedding it into the organization. The company enhances change capacity by strengthening a sustainable internal culture and by forming new relationships with externals. The company develops an engagement strategy which leads to building out the vision across the organization that it is shared by all. As people across the company make the vision their own, adding to its richness, the new identity also comes into clearer focus.

Transformational change is radical and requires a vision and commitment from the top-level leader of the organization. It requires a high tolerance for ambiguity, perseverance, and courage. Those who wish to lead it must be willing to examine their own capacity for change and become open to personal transformation. And while there are no sure paths to transformation, the action learning process has been demonstrated to be effective in leading transformational change.

Your turn: assessing your company

As you think about your company and your own personal circumstances, what are your reactions to change and transformation? Respond to the questions below to stimulate your thinking.

Step 1: organizational reflection on sustainability

Is your company sustainable?	
What is your company's approach to sustainability? Is it ignoring it? Is it trying to do less harm? Do more good? Other?	
What do you think your company is trying to achieve by engaging with sustainability? For example, create good will with the shareholders? Engage employees? Create a good reputation with the public? Save money and minimize risks? Contribute to the common good? Other?	
How would you rate your company in comparison with others in the industry regarding becoming sustainable?	
How would you rate your company's leaders compared with other leaders in your industry in their commitment to becoming sustainable?	

Does your top-level leader have a vision for becoming more sustainable? If so, what is it?	
Do you believe that becoming sustainable is part of your company's identity? If so, describe how.	
What steps do you think your company should take to become more sustainable?	
What, if anything, can you do to inspire/ move your company to become more sustainable?	
What kinds of conversations should take place inside your company pertaining to becoming more sustainable? Who should lead them? Who should participate?	

Step 2: transformational change

Do you think that your company's culture needs to change? If so, how?	
Describe either a change or transformation in your organization that you have experienced. What did it look like? Did it succeed?	
Do you believe that transformation is important for your organization? Why or why not?	
Is your company on the Transformational Cycle? If so, at what stage? What are your observations so far as to how it is working, or not working, for the company?	
Do you believe that your company handles incremental change well? Why or why not?	

How could incremental change move your company towards becoming more sustainable?	
What can you contribute to creating incremental change towards becoming more sustainable?	

Step 3: personal transformation (only for those of you who are interested in becoming transformational leaders)

Where can you seek support to develop your own capacities for personal change and transformation?	
What, if anything, would you like to learn about becoming a transformational leader?	
What steps will you take towards developing into a transformational leader?	
What are your thoughts and plans for next steps now that you have finished reading this book?	

Notes

1 Robert Eccles, Kathleen Miller Perkins, and George Serafeim, "How to Become a Sustainable Company," *MIT Sloan Management Review*, (Summer 2012), 53, no. 4, 43–50. Available at: https://sloanreview.mit.edu/article/how-to-become-a-sustainable-company.

2 Eccles, Miller Perkins, and Serafeim, 2012, 50.

3 Jim Harter and Anna Marie Mann, "The Right Culture: Not Just About Employee Satisfaction," *Gallup Business Journal*, April 2017. Available at: www.gallup.com/workplace/236366/right-culture-not-employee-satisfaction.aspx.

4 Kathleen Miller Perkins and George Serafeim, "Chief Sustainability Officers: Who are They and What do They Do?" in *Leading Sustainable Change*, eds Rebecca Henderson, Ranjay Gulati, and Michael Tushman (Oxford, UK: Oxford University Press, 2015), 196–221.

5 Paul Hawkins, *The Ecology of Commerce* (New York: Harper Business, 1993).

6 Ray Anderson with Robin White, *Business Lessons from a Radical Industrialist* (New York: St. Martin's Press, 2009–2010).

7 PepsiCo website, accessed on September 7, 2018. Available at: www.pepsico.com/sustainability/performance-with-purpose.

8 Robert Quinn, *Building the Bridge as You Walk on It* (Jossey-Bass, 2008).

9 Robert Gass, "What is Transformational Change?" (pdf, Hidden Leaf Foundation, 2010). Available at: http://hiddenleaf.electricembers.net/wp-content/uploads/2010/06/What-is-Transformational-Change.pdf.

10 Jenny Davis-Peccoud, Paul Stone, and Clare Tovey, "Achieving Breakthrough Results in Sustainability," Bain & Company, 2016. Available at: www.transparantiebenchmark.nl/sites/transparantiebenchmark.nl/files/afbeeldingen/achieving_breakthrough_results_in_sustainability_bain_brief.pdf.

11 Kathleen Miller and Shari Lewchanin, "Getting Ready to Get Ready for Change," *Consulting to Management Journal*, (September, 2001), 12, no. 3, 42–44.

12 David Rooke and William Torbert, "Seven Transformations of Leadership," *Harvard Business Review*, (April 2015), 66–77.

13 Bill Torbert and Associates, *Action Inquiry: The Secret of Timely and Transforming Leadership* (San Francisco: Berrett-Koehler Publishers, 2004).

14 Quinn, 2008.

15 World Institute for Action Learning website, accessed on September 8, 2018. Available at: https://wial.org/action-learning.

16 Arthur Freedman, "Using Action Learning for Organizational Development and Change," *OD Practitioner*, (2011), 43, no. 2, 1–12. Available at: https://c.ymcdn.com/sites/www.odnetwork.org/resource/resmgr/publications/371.pdf.

17 Christopher Juniper, "Action Research and The Sustainability Imperative," in *Cooking with Action Research: Stories and Resources for Self and Community Transformation*, ed. Bradbury and Associates (2017), 10.

18 William Torbert website, accessed September 8, 2018. Available at: www.williamrtorbert.com/action-inquiry.

Afterword

As I have written this book, I have reflected on my own path both personally and professionally over the course of my career. My company, Miller Consultants, has gone through a transformation much like those I have described in this book.

The transformation of Miller Consultants Inc. was prompted by a crisis that almost sank the company, and an experience that opened my eyes to a new way of doing business. In the mid-1990s we were a successful small business. I had started the company in 1980 with an idealistic vision. I wanted to help other corporations create a culture where employees could apply their knowledge, strengths, and creativity to engage in meaningful work. I had a strong desire, as a social psychologist, to pursue this path. However, over the years I tended to take the company wherever the dollars beckoned. We began to offer mostly management training and instructional design assistance to just about anyone who could pay for it. I fell into the trap of focusing almost exclusively on growth and profits. As a result, I structured my organization around a business model that was common for professional services firms such as law practices and consultancies. I assigned sales quotas to the people who worked for me, and I expected them to work very long hours, sacrificing their own personal and family needs. We charged our clients by the hour and looked for ways to maximize our fees including the common practice of leveraging the work of junior people who were paid lower salaries.

Our culture shifted from the collaborative workplace we had nurtured originally to a competitive environment where trust and camaraderie were low. Turnover was high and the employees who remained were unhappy. We were profitable, but I had lost my passion for the work and everyone knew it. Morale plummeted. And then we faced a crisis. One of our long-time employees embezzled a large sum of money from the company. By the time we discovered it, we were practically bankrupt. I was so discouraged that I planned to shut down the company as soon as I found a new career. Yet I trudged on for a few years, trying to find my way even as the company lost most of our team.

At my lowest point, we acquired a client with a fresh perspective that was new to me. The client was a hydro-electric company in Canada that talked about a commitment to a triple bottom line – people, planet, and profit. I saw this organization balance their quest to make a profit with their desire to

serve society. As I learned more about this business model, I became reinvig-
orated and envisioned how my own company could live its original purpose
while also making a profit. I determined that Miller Consultants would once
again become a purpose-driven company. My new vision built on where I
had started many years earlier. I wanted Miller Consultants to assist organizations in building cultures where employees are engaged in meaningful work
which contributes to the company's success and to the betterment of the
world. This meant that our company would need to transform. Today we
describe our purpose as helping others create sustainable cultures built on
collaboration and contribution.

Vision alone wasn't enough. This transformation to renewed purpose
required other changes as well. We realized that we had to realign our work
and the services we provided. My team collaborated with me to determine
what this purpose and vision would mean for us going forward. One of our
first decisions was to accept client engagements only when we felt we could
truly have a positive impact on employee well-being and company performance. That meant giving up the delivery of training that had little chance of
creating real change for the participants and their organizations. This resolve
meant that we had to make some hard choices about turning down work
which would have been lucrative but did not fit our criteria.

The transformation of the company has been ongoing for a decade. Over
that time, we have faced many pitfalls. From time to time we have fallen back
into bad habits only to pick ourselves up and look for a new way to move
forward. Transforming the company is still a work in progress. The process of
identifying and addressing the discrepancies between what we stand for and
how we act has led us to engage in all types of change. For example, I now
take more risks in service to our vision and potential long-term gain. None
of us hesitates to talk about values, even with audiences where the message
may be unpopular. We make decisions collaboratively, including what we
charge our clients and how much each team member is paid. We design our
projects together with thought to how each team member involved can best
use her strengths. Our renewed cultural foundation clearly guides our work.
Nevertheless, the transformation has been difficult, and it is certainly not over.

As you think about the issues that you face in your own organizations,
please share your thoughts and experiences with me. I find that I am at my best
when I am interacting with others and learning from them as well as sharing
what I have learned. I believe that we are all in this together. We all want our
work to be meaningful and we all want to make a difference. Let's support
each other, teach each other, and learn from each other.

Appendix
Research methodology overview

This ongoing research program led by the author, Kathleen Miller Perkins of Miller Consultants, began in 2008. While the research teams' membership varied over the studies, those who have participated include Robert Eccles, Harvard Business School, George Serafeim, Harvard Business School, Meredith Lepley, Miller Consultants and University of Southern California, Katrin Muff, formerly Dean of Business School of Lausanne, and Kathleen Miller Perkins, Miller Consultants and formerly Virginia Tech University and Business School of Lausanne.

In 2008 through 2010 we interviewed practitioners, academics, and others either interested in or studying the issues pertaining to sustainability and culture. At the same time, we began a thorough review of the literature and the survey research reports. In 2010 we were engaged by a client organization to conduct a study of how their culture related to their sustainability goals. We constructed a survey instrument to use in this work. We worked with another consulting organization which measured more technical aspects of the company's sustainability work and results. Together we presented our data to the client company and assisted them in designing a roadmap to guide their future sustainability efforts. One of the most interesting findings in this initial work was that the employees whose work connected the most closely to sustainability were the most engaged. This pattern has shown up in all our subsequent studies. Based on our work with this client company, we began our empirical studies of sustainability and organizational culture in 2011.

Study 1

Method

Using the survey we had designed for our client in 2010 as our template, we designed an assessment instrument composed of items pertaining to culture and leadership. In addition to the information we obtained through our own work, we used the data from our review of the public literature and material we obtained through interviews with experts in the field. While much of the survey literature focused on aspects of sustainability other than culture and leadership, many works included at least one or two items relevant to our study. Therefore, to construct our instrument, we gathered the data from across many surveys. Each item in the assessment described in this report is tied to a specific survey item or derived from a model or a characteristic that we uncovered in our research reviews and interviews. The assessment contains both sustainability-specific content as well as more general organizational climate content that has been demonstrated or asserted in other research to impact the execution of sustainability strategy.

The instrument that we administered in this study was composed of the following categories of questions:

Organizational leadership

Organizational leadership refers to those who are in formal positions of authority from the executives at the top of the organization down through the management ranks.

Organizational systems

Organizational systems are the mechanisms through which work is regulated and results are measured and communicated.

Organizational climate

Organizational climate is defined as the characteristics of the internal environment as experienced by its members. It can influence behavior and can be described in terms of a set of characteristics of the organization such as ability to collaborate or levels of trust.

Change readiness

Change readiness is defined as the organization's ability to implement and sustain change.

Internal stakeholders

Internal stakeholders are groups or individuals within the bounds of the organization who can affect or are affected by the achievement of the sustainability objectives.

External stakeholders

External stakeholders are groups or individuals outside the organization who can affect or are affected by the achievement of the sustainability objectives.

About the sample

The sample included 53 people representing 32 companies. Participants came from public (43 percent) and private (47 percent) organizations as well as a few from not for profits. Participants tended to be senior-level managers or above (63 percent), and represented a wide range of functions including operations, corporate responsibility, marketing, environmental affairs, finance, supply chain, and communications. We invited two types of companies to participate and assigned them to groups before they took the survey based on the following criteria.

Early Adopters

We defined *Early Adopters* as organizations highlighted in the press, articles, and indices as being leaders in sustainability. We contacted these companies to ask them to participate and to confirm the following: Whether they saw their organizations as sustainability leaders and upon what basis they made this claim. These organizations included companies such as IBM, Kaiser Permanente, UPS, and others known at the time for aggressively pursuing sustainability goals. Also, we included organizations with experts in sustainability, i.e., people who have been in the forefront of innovative practices and research. We invited up to three people per company in each group to participate. A total of 33 people representing 17 *Early Adopters* organizations took the assessment. Most of the organizations in this sample are either very large (53 percent employed over 10,000) or small (41 percent employed under 500).

Others

In addition to the *Early Adopters*, we contacted companies in our network that had not been singled out by the press and/or in articles for their sustainability leadership. We invited three people from each of these companies to participate in the survey pilot. We refer to these companies as *Others*. A total of 20 people from 15 companies in this category took the assessment.

In addition to assigning the companies to the two categories a priori, we also included some questions on the survey itself that helped us check on the validity of the sample assignment. We looked at responses to items such as the breadth of companies' definitions of sustainability and the degree to which they have mechanisms in place to measure operational performance and compliance in the areas generally associated with sustainability strategy. We used these data to validate the sample assignment. We found that the companies which we had assigned to the Early Adopter category did, in fact, show more leadership in sustainability based on their answers.

Study 2: Eccles, Miller Perkins, and Serafeim

Methodology

We continued to review the existing literature on the relationship of organizational culture and corporate sustainability. Based on the themes, we interviewed approximately 200 people from leading corporations to examine the aspects of organizational culture that they found to be important to implementing their sustainability strategies.

This preliminary research revealed some interesting patterns that we decided to explore with a revised survey. Based on these preliminary data and Study 1 described above, we designed a 68-item assessment instrument that we refer to as the SCALA™ (Sustainability Culture and Leadership Assessment). The instrument looked at leadership, organizational systems and climate, change readiness, and internal and external stakeholders. We examined the sustainability performance on both environmental and social factors for 3,000+ companies worldwide for 2009, with data provided by Thomson Reuters' ASSET4. We isolated the top 20 percent and the bottom 20 percent of companies in terms of environmental and social performance. Then we imposed an additional filter, isolating companies from both the top and bottom groups based on whether they integrate social and environmental metrics and narrative with their financial reporting. We identified 58 companies with good sustainability performance and 108 with poor sustainability performance. We invited these companies to take the survey. We found significant differences between the groups in approximately half of the 68 items. We validated the results of the survey through interviews with experts in sustainability.[1]

After this second study, we revised the survey assessment instrument based on our findings and have administered it to over 4,000 people in over 200 companies as of 2018. Beginning in 2019, we are revising the organization of the survey into the following categories: Leadership, Identity, Trust, Internal Organizational Culture, External Relationships, Change and Innovation. We plan to keep all the current scales in the revised version of the SCALA and to add some additional items that have come to light recently as we study how sustainable companies' cultures differ from others.

Study 3: chief sustainability officers: who are they and what do they do?

In 2015, in partnership with George Serafeim, we conducted a survey of Chief Sustainability Officers (CSOs) to ascertain how their companies approach sustainability and to find out more about their roles. We obtained our sample of 130 participants through announcements on-line. We were able to look at the stages that companies go through in their sustainability journey and to identify how the roles of both the CEO and the CSO changed throughout the stages.[2]

Study 4: meta-analysis[3]

Methodology

In 2016, we carried out a meta-analysis that included all the data in our data base (3,000+ participants) to look for trends and relationships among the concepts measured. In addition, we performed several regression analyses to determine the direction of these relationships, e.g., which variables seem to lead to engagement, and how do the leadership characteristics and behaviors affect other perceptions of the culture as well as commitments to sustainability.

Study 5: meta-analysis of the cultures as categorized by the Dyllick and Muff typology[4]

Methodology

In 2018, we carried out a meta-analysis of data in which we compared companies assigned to the following three categories based on the typology developed by Dyllick and Muff:

1   **Business Sustainability 1.0** – "A first step in introducing sustainability into the current economic paradigm results from recognizing that there are new business challenges from exchanges that are outside of the market. Extra-market challenges result from environmental or social concerns which are typically voiced by external stakeholders like NGOs, media, legislation, or government. They raise environmental and social concerns that create economic risks and opportunities for business. These new challenges are picked up and integrated into existing processes and practices without changing the basic business premise and outlook. Even if sustainability concerns are considered in decision making and actions, business objectives remain clearly focused on creating shareholder value."[5]
2   **Triple Bottom Line** – "Those that broadened the stakeholder perspective and incorporated commitments to the triple bottom line, including environmental, social and financial concerns. Value creation goes beyond shareholder value and includes social and environmental values. Companies create value not just as a side effect of their business activities, but as the result of deliberately defined goals and programs addressed at specific sustainability issues or stakeholders."[6]
3   **Truly Sustainable Business** – "Truly sustainable business shifts its perspective from seeking to minimize its negative impacts to understanding how it can create a significant positive impact in critical and relevant areas for society."[7]

General research

Through the years we have continued to carry out more qualitative research, including archival research, interviews, and case studies, to expand our understanding of the cultures of self-identified as well as some certified purpose-driven companies.

Research findings: overall summary

Sustainable companies have been shown to outperform their counterparts in the stock market and on other financial variables such as return on assets and return on equity.[8] Moreover, the culture of sustainable companies differs from others as well in terms of their identity and how it guides their behaviors, their assumptions and mindsets, how they treat their employees, and how they relate to stakeholders outside their own boundaries.

Company identity and mental models/mindsets tend to be distinct in the most socially responsible businesses and these foundational components tend to guide behaviors and decisions more than in other companies. They are more likely to clearly define their role in terms of their responsibilities to society. They tend to have an outside-in mindset, meaning that they look first at trends and challenges in their communities, if not throughout the world, and then assess how they might channel their own internal capabilities to address these external issues.

Sustainable companies have a more positive internal workplace environment than their less sustainable counterparts. Their vigorous work to create a culture of trust pays off. Not only do they have a more engaged workforce than other companies, their high levels of trust mean that their efforts to enable cross-functional collaboration and idea exchange also succeed. They have stronger commitments to reflect on and learn from their own experiences as well as from people outside their organizations.

These companies have clear strategies for engaging employees. They communicate the impact that each employee's work has on the company as well as how the work is connected to their sustainability goals and purpose. Their employees are indeed more highly engaged than those in other companies. The greater the company commitment to sustainability, the higher the levels of employee engagement.

Sustainable companies differ from others in how they relate to people and organizations outside their own boundaries. They care about their reputation with the public and encourage their employees to learn from externals. They collaborate with other organizations such as NGOs, universities, and even their own competitors to extend their own capabilities and to tackle problems that they cannot solve on their own. They are more likely than others to encourage sustainability in their supply chain.

Leaders in sustainable companies have a clearer vision pertaining to their purpose and sustainable goals. The strength of their business case for sustainability supports the power of their vision as viewed by others. They communicate the company's commitment to purpose and to sustainability simply and consistently to the world outside their traditional boundaries. In fact, leaders with the richest visions encourage others within the company to learn from the outside.

Leaders' personal commitments and ability to inspire lend power to the vision. They make their visions "come alive" in the organization through such things as embedding purpose and sustainable values into operations and linking rewards and compensation to their sustainability goals. They communicate a clear and consistent message externally as well. They tend to take a long-term view when setting strategies and they integrate purpose and sustainable values into their decision-making.

Sustainable companies are more change-adept. They have stronger track records for both small incremental changes as well as large-scale changes. Their leaders are more willing to take risks – a quality important to change of any kind. They encourage people to challenge the status quo and support and reinforce innovation.

Our research shows that some companies begin a transformational change process due to a leader's break with the mental models that have defined the organization. Other times leaders reach the point of desiring transformation more gradually and go through several other types of change first. In either case, once the leader commits to transformation, she initiates the change by crafting a vision. The transformation unfolds through the social interactions throughout the organization leading to a shared vision and action. Often the CEO designates responsibility for facilitating the process to a change agent – another high-level leader in a centralized role – often in a new position that the CEO creates, such as a Chief Sustainability Officer. Nevertheless, the CEO retains sponsorship of the transformation while the change agent, no matter what the official title, oversees the development and implementation of the strategies. In large organizations, the timing of the transformational process varies in different parts of the company. The change agent's role is to assist with the customization of the grand plan to the local needs as the entire company begins to transform.[9]

The big picture in sustainable companies is that they are more successful in engaging external stakeholders and employees. Their cultures are built on a strong identity, unique leadership, and trust. Moreover, their cultures support innovation and they have a stronger track-record for handling change.[10] Finally, their employees are more engaged than in other organizations.

Notes

1 Robert Eccles, Kathleen Miller Perkins, and George Serafeim, "How to Become a Sustainable Company," *MIT Sloan Management Review*, (Summer 2012), 53, no. 4, 43–50.
2 Kathleen Miller Perkins and George Serafeim, "Chief Sustainability Officers: Who are They and What do They Do?" in *Leading Sustainable Change*, eds Rebecca Henderson, Ranjay Gulati, and Michael Tushman (Oxford, UK: Oxford University Press, 2015), 196–221.
3 Kathleen Perkins and Meredith Lepley, "Meta Data Analysis of Sustainability Culture and Leadership Assessment (SCALA)," unpublished manuscript, 2016.
4 Katrin Muff, Kathleen Miller Perkins, Meredith Lepley, and Agnieszka Kapalka, "Culture Differences Between Business as Usual and Sustainable Companies," Working Paper, 2018.

5 Thomas Dyllick and Katrin Muff, "Clarifying the Meaning of Sustainable Business: Introducing a Typology From Business-as-Usual to True Business Sustainability." *Organization and Environment Journal*, (2016), 29, no. 2, 156–174.

6 Dyllick and Muff, 2016, 164.

7 Dyllick and Muff, 2016, 165.

8 Robert Eccles, Ioannis Ioannou, and George Serafeim, "The Impact of Corporate Sustainability on Organizational Processes and Performance," (written December 23, 2014), *Management Science*, 60, no. 11 (published February 2014): 2835–2857. Available at: https://ssrn.com/abstract=1964011 or http://dx.doi.org/10.2139/ssrn.1964011.

9 Miller Perkins and Serafeim, 196–221.

10 Eccles, Miller Perkins, and Serafeim, 43–50.

Index